Matthew's Gospel from Scratch

Matthew's Gospel from Scratch

The New Testament for Beginners

Donald L. Griggs
Earl S. Johnson, Jr.

WESTMINSTER
JOHN KNOX PRESS
LOUISVILLE · KENTUCKY

First edition
Published by Westminster John Knox Press
Louisville, Kentucky

11 12 13 14 15 16 17 18 19 20—10 9 8 7 6 5 4 3 2 1

Book design by Teri Kays Vinson
Cover design by Night & Day Design

Library of Congress Cataloging-in-Publication Data

Griggs, Donald L.
  Matthew's Gospel from scratch : the New Testament for beginners / Donald L. Griggs, Earl S. Johnson, Jr.
      p. cm.
  Includes bibliographical references.
  ISBN 978-0-664-23485-0 (alk. paper)
  1. Bible. N.T. Matthew—Textbooks. 2. Bible. N.T. Matthew—Study and teaching. I. Johnson, Earl S., 1942- II. Title.
  BS2576.G75 2010
  226.2'061—dc22

                                                                2010034954

PRINTED IN THE UNITED STATES OF AMERICA

♾ The paper used in this publication meets the minimum requirements of the American National Standard for Information Sciences—Permanence of Paper for Printed Library Materials, ANSI Z39.48-1992

Westminster John Knox Press advocates the responsible use of our natural resources. The text paper of this book is made from 30% post-consumer waste.

Most Westminster John Knox Press books are available at special quantity discounts when purchased in bulk by corporations, organizations, and special-interest groups. For more information, please e-mail SpecialSales@wjkbooks.com.

Contents

Contents

Part One

PARTICIPANT'S GUIDE

EARL S. JOHNSON, JR.

Preface to Part One

The First Book

For many Christians Matthew is the first Gospel they read simply because it is the first book in the New Testament. Certainly that was the case for me. I started studying it seriously when I was in college, and I was fascinated by the vital stories about Jesus' teaching and actions found there. For many years it has remained the Gospel I turn to when I try to understand who Jesus is and what he has to say to me today.

Matthew was the subject of my first Bible class when I worked as a seminary student with junior high youth in Newark, New Jersey, and I have preached through parts of it many times in the four different churches I have served since then. When I was working on my doctoral dissertation on Mark's Gospel, I became interested in the similarities and differences between Matthew's presentation of Jesus and the one found in Mark. I still find it exciting to try and figure out why Matthew changed his source the way he did. So when Don Griggs invited me to write a volume in this new series, I quickly chose Matthew's Gospel and could hardly wait to get started.

Why Is Matthew the First Book in the New Testament?

It seems logical to begin reading any book like the New Testament at the beginning. But why *is* Matthew the first Gospel when the church had three others to select? And why is it the first writing in the whole New Testament when there are twenty-six other choices? Why not put Paul's letter to the Romans first, the Acts of the Apostles, or the first epistle of John?

According to the church historian Eusebius, the bishop of Caesarea who lived around 263–339 CE, a number of considerations caused the early church to give it front-page recognition.

1. Christians believed, Eusebius said, that it was the first of the Gospels to be written and therefore the oldest, and by implication the most reliable.

2. Papias (ca. 60–130 CE) wrote that Matthew was of primary importance because it contained the actual sayings (Gk., *logia*) of Jesus himself, written in the Hebrew (Aramaic) language.

3. Eusebius also points out that later writers went on to argue that the first Gospel was written by a person who should really know what Jesus said, namely, Matthew, who was not only a disciple but also an apostle, one who wrote a message for the Hebrews while Peter and Paul were preaching in Rome and forming the church there.[1] The comment that Matthew was an apostle is significant because the first Christians placed high priority on the witness and writings of those who were the actual disciples of Jesus and were apostles appointed by him after the resurrection (like Paul was on the Damascus road in Acts 9), or knew Jesus' disciples (like Mark did).

What Is the Understanding of Matthew's Importance Today?

Since the time when Eusebius compiled his information about the formation of the New Testament, a great deal has been learned about the background of the Gospels and times in which they were written. Today, for example, it is known from careful comparisons and contrasts of the first three Gospels that Matthew was not the first Gospel written after all. In fact, Matthew and Luke both used Mark's Gospel for a model and source to write their accounts. Mark's story of Jesus is actually the first and the oldest. Matthew and Luke also had access to another collection of sayings of Jesus that circulated throughout the church (called the Q document), as well as their own individual sources of information (often referred to as M and L). Neither of them, however, appears to have been aware of the work of the other.

It is also unlikely that the whole book was written first in Aramaic. Although Jesus and the disciples certainly spoke that first-century CE version of Hebrew (the one used in the movie *The Passion of Christ* produced by Mel Gibson in 2004), and it is evident that some verses are a translation of an earlier Aramaic version, many scholars now think that Matthew was originally written in Greek (the international language of diplomacy and business) so that more people could read it throughout the Roman Empire. Since one of the main purposes of Matthew was to make disciples in the name of the Father and the Son and the Holy Spirit throughout the world (28:16–20), it would make sense to put it in the language most people could understand.

Today, of course, there are other reasons why Matthew is of primary importance to Christians and why it is still on a Christian best-seller list. For one thing, the main themes in Matthew are especially valuable now as Christians struggle to maintain their faith at a time in history that is filled with violence, political intrigue, and racial and ethnic prejudice. It is worth reading again as the world faces severe economic recession and as the church struggles with diminishing attendance and membership in many places, leading some to think that belief in God and commitment to the kingdom of heaven is declining in an increasingly secularized society. Matthew is also significant to readers in the twenty-first century for a number of other reasons:

- The emphasis that the first Christians placed on the Old Testament and the way it can be understood afresh in light of Jesus' life and ministry and their appreciation of the unity of the Scriptures

- The ethical values that Jesus taught in the Sermon on the Mount (chaps. 5–7) and the new interpretation he gave to the Ten Commandments for a new day

- The importance of the church's ministry to the poor, the sick, the aliens, and the lost and the reasons that its ministry can only occur through strong and resilient faith (chaps. 8–13)

- The process that Matthew describes that can be used to solve internal problems in churches today and run them more effectively and powerfully (chap. 18)

- Jesus' example of how to respond to systemic religious and political oppression by showing how he resisted the

power of the elite religious leaders in Jerusalem as well
as the Roman government and military officials who
occupied the whole country (chaps. 1–2, 14–27)[2]

• The absolute importance of mission in all times and
places (chap. 28) as the church reaches out to those
who say no to Jesus (Jews and Gentiles alike) and why,
on the basis of the Old Testament, and the truth about
Jesus' identity as God's Son, they should say yes.[3]

What Kind of a Book Is Matthew?

Although Matthew is usually referred to as a *Gospel* in the inscription added to
Bibles today, the author himself simply calls his work *a book* in 1:1. The Greek
word for book there is *biblos* and is translated in the New Revised Standard
Version of the Bible (NRSV) as "an account." It can also refer to the type of
manuscript it was, that is, a text written on a document with pages that could
be turned rather than on a piece of papyrus that had to be unrolled to be read.
John uses the same word to describe his work (John 20:30; 21:25), and it is from
biblos that the English word *Bible* is derived. Mark calls what he writes a *gospel*
(Mark 1:1), but that term is reserved in Matthew for the preaching of Jesus (usually translated "good news," 4:23; 9:35; 24:14; 26:13). *Gospel* was applied later
to all four of the first books of the New Testament, but it was not one used by
Matthew, Luke, or John to describe their own works.

What kind of book was it? Although the author appears to present a history of Jesus' life, ministry, death, and resurrection, his intention is much
more than that. Rather than trying to write a biography of Jesus in the modern
sense, Matthew was composed as a message to the church, particularly Jewish
Christians, about what it means to follow Jesus, understand the Old Testament
in a new way, maintain faith in a hostile and dangerous world, and forge ahead
with ministry and mission, no matter what happens.

As William Barclay put it, there are two ways to tell a story. One tries to get
all the facts in order, detail by detail, day by day, week by week, attempting to
leave nothing out. The other takes a series of significant incidents and episodes
and uses them as windows to see into the mind and heart of a person one is seeking to know. It is this second way that Matthew uses in his book. As Barclay
says, it is like the difference between a photograph and a portrait. A photograph
reproduces what a person looks like in every detail. A portrait is designed to
reveal inner character and special qualities. Thus Matthew can be said to be a
portrait. It is not just a description of Jesus; it is an invitation to see the mind of
God in him and believe in him as the Son of God to whom the whole of life must
be given.[4] Rather than trying to read Matthew as a precise historical presentation

of what Jesus said and did, one will find it more instructive to see it as a careful description of who he is and what it means to follow him.

The Author

According to the inscription of the book that was added later, the author's name is Matthew. Early Christians believed that its author was the Matthew who had been a tax collector (9:9–13; 10:3) and changed his life when he met Jesus (see Mark 2:13–17 and Luke 5:27–32, where the name Levi is used). He is mentioned again in Acts 1:13 as one of the eleven remaining disciples (after Judas's death) when a meeting was held in an upper room in Jerusalem. Ancient church traditions say that he died as a martyr in Pontus, Persia, or Ethiopia. Modern scholars are not certain that one author wrote or edited the entire book, but the name Matthew was attached to it by the early church to give it importance as one written by a disciple of Jesus. Whoever wrote it, the author or a final editor, Matthew was certainly one who was deeply committed to Jesus Christ, was concerned about Jewish resistance to him, was open to a broad mission to Gentiles, and was dedicated to the careful formation of a fledgling church during tumultuous and perilous times.

When Was the Book Written and Who Were Its Readers?

Because of the concern expressed throughout Matthew about the harsh opposition inveighed against Jesus by the Jewish leaders in both Galilee and Jerusalem, and because of Jesus' resistance to Roman oppression, most scholars think that Matthew's Gospel was written sometime after the fall of Jerusalem and the rest of Palestine to the Roman generals Vespasian and Titus in 70 CE and the years following. Such a date locates the writing of the book several years after Paul's death and the writing of Mark, and a few years prior to John, and about the same time as the composition of Luke, probably somewhere in the time frame from 80–90 CE. Although it is clear that the book was sent to people who were Jewish Christian in background (Jews who had converted to Christianity), it is not certain where they lived. Suggestions have been made that it may have been written for a church in one of the large cities in Galilee (Sepphoris or Tiberias), in Syria (perhaps Antioch), in Caesarea Maritima on the west coast of Palestine, or maybe even in Damascus.

Wherever Matthew's readers lived, it is likely that they had experienced a time of terrible chaos after the Romans had invaded city after city. During this period the Jews were struggling with their identity now that their Temple in the capital and many of their meeting places (synagogues) elsewhere had been destroyed, and the church, as chapter 18 shows, was working hard to establish itself (often in competition with Judaism) and to bring its message to Jews and Gentiles alike. Truly, it was a trying period when Christians had to move beyond "little faith" (8:26; 17:20) to the powerful trust that could move mountains of fear and doubt (21:21).

Notes

1. Eusebius, in *Ecclesiastical History*, not only cites Papias but also Ireneus (around 130–200 CE) and Origen (around 185–254 CE).
2. I am indebted to the careful research of Warren Carter for this insight. See *Matthew and the Margins: A Sociopolitical and Religious Reading, Initial Explorations* (Maryknoll, NY: Orbis Books, 2000); and *Matthew and Empire* (Harrisburg, PA: Trinity Press International, 2001).
3. According to Ulrich Luz, "The Gospel of Matthew is a response to the no of Israel's majority to Jesus. It is the attempt to come to terms with this no by defining the community's position and to contribute to forming and preserving its identity in a situation of crisis and transition" *(Matthew 1–7*, Hermenia [Minneapolis: Fortress Press, 2007], 55).
4. William Barclay, *Introducing the Bible* (Nashville: Abingdon Press, 1972, 1979), 52.

Chapter One

Family Tree, Birth, and Early Life of Jesus

A Study of Matthew 1:1–2:23

Jesus' Family Tree (1:1–17)

It is not surprising that Matthew begins with a genealogy outlining Jesus' lineage. In ancient cultures, oral lists of a person's family tree were often memorized and passed down from generation to generation so that no one would forget one's ancestral background. In a television series popular in 1977, viewers saw how such a tradition worked in Africa in the story of Kunta Kinte adapted from Alex Haley's novel *Roots*.

In 1:1–17 Jesus' roots are traced back to King David. Matthew is keen to show that Jesus is not just the son of a carpenter and a young woman but that he is king's-blood royal ("the Messiah," v. 17). He goes further to extend the lines all the way back to Abraham because this founder of Israel was promised by God: " 'I will make of you a great nation, and I will bless you, and make your name great, so that you will be a blessing. I will bless those who bless you, and the one who curses you I will curse; and in you all the families of the earth shall be blessed.' " (Gen. 12:2–3). A similar genealogy in the Old Testament traces

David's family to Adam, the first man (1 Chron. 1–2). Luke does the same thing for Jesus in his report about Jesus' childhood (Luke 3:23–38).

The different ways in which the two Gospel writers trace Jesus' lineage are worth noting. Matthew brings it through his legal father, Joseph, whereas Luke focuses on Mary's family tree. The divergence probably occurs because it was not clear how the writers should regard Jesus' unique virgin birth. If Joseph was not his biological father, should he be called the Son of Joseph or not? Matthew thinks he should and stays within the normal Jewish tradition (see Matt. 13:55, "Is this not the carpenter's son?"). With his introduction, however, Matthew goes one step further. Since Joseph is a "Son of David" (1:20), Jesus can claim this title as well (9:27; 12:23; 22:42).

In this family tree, moreover, Matthew does not worry about being precise chronologically. Although there were more than forty-two generations between Jesus and Abraham, Matthew may have adopted the formula of three fourteen-member groups for symbolic purposes (1:17). He also includes more than Jewish men in his outline, listing four Gentile women: Tamar (v. 3), Ruth (v. 5), Rahab (v. 5), and Bathsheba ("the wife of Uriah," v. 6). No doubt he wants to demonstrate that Jesus is the savior of all people and all the nations, non-Jews and Jews alike, as well as both women and men, as the key verse in Matthew 28:19 demonstrates. What is more, since three of the women (Tamar, Rahab, and Bathsheba) and many of the men all have unsavory backgrounds, it is clear that Matthew is not trying to "doctor" Jesus' family tree to make it appear purer than it really is.

Two key words appear in this section that need to be defined. Matthew begins and ends it by referring to Jesus as *Messiah*. In Greek the word *Christos* means "the anointed one," "someone ordained by God for a specific duty." In Jesus' case the first Christians believed that he was the one called by God to fulfill Jewish expectations that one would come who would save God's people (Rom. 9:5; 1 Thess. 1:11; 5:9; Gal. 1:4; 1 Cor. 1:8). Throughout the Gospel various people debate what that means until Jesus appears to claim the title for himself on the cross (Matt. 26:64; 27:11).

Deportation (v. 17) refers to the time of the exile, when the Jews were driven out of their homeland and were forced to live as refugees in Babylon for forty years (see 2 Kgs. 24:8–25:30 and the books of Ezra and Nehemiah) until they were allowed to return and rebuild Jerusalem.

The Story of Jesus' Unique Birth and Modern Interpretations (1:18–21)

Matthew's story of Jesus' birth has created many wonderful memories for millions of Christians over the centuries. Believers can remember past Christmas eves: the singing of favorite carols, the lighting of candles, and perhaps even snow on the ground after services were over.

A close examination of Matthew's text demonstrates, however, that his account is not quite as romantic as readers might expect. The tension created between a husband and wife when Joseph suspects Mary of adultery, the brutal political intrigue of King Herod many months after Jesus' birth, the necessary deception of the magi, and the forced flight of the first family to Egypt (a kind of reverse exodus) make Matthew's story more like a modern murder mystery than a Christmas-card portrait. Nevertheless, despite the challenging aspects of the story of Jesus' birth, Matthew's major emphasis remains: in Jesus Christ God is with us and the world is changed because he came.

Culturally it is necessary to understand the relationship between Joseph and Mary. In the first century CE it was customary for a young girl to be engaged to a man at an early age. Presumably Joseph was much older, for he already had children from a previous marriage (see references to Jesus' siblings, Matt. 12:46–50; 13:55; Mark 3:21, 31–35; 6:3; John 7:5), and tradition indicates that he probably died when Jesus was still young. Many scholars think that Mary was probably around fifteen years old or even younger when they were "engaged." In Matthew's story, when she becomes pregnant by the Holy Spirit (1:18), Joseph thinks she is guilty of adultery. Legally she could be charged, sentenced, and stoned to death. Being a decent man, however, Joseph decides to "divorce" her quietly, and it takes the word of an angel (a messenger from God) to convince him that her pregnancy is indeed miraculous.

O Come, O Come, Emmanuel (1:22–25)

For Matthew the miracle does not come out of the blue. It is a fulfillment of an Old Testament prophecy, the first of many that will be seen throughout his report (look at 2:6, 18; 4:4, 6, 15, etc., for other examples). For the early Christians, when it could be demonstrated that an event had been previously envisioned by a prophet, it was clear to them that it was truly happening according to God's will. In the case of Jesus' birth, Matthew sees a parallel in Isaiah 7:14 (and Isa. 8:8) in the account of a young woman who is to bear a child as a sign of God's grace and power.

For modern Christians, the connection between the Old and New Testaments may not be quite as clear as it was for Matthew and his readers, and many people today struggle with the fact that the prophecy in Isaiah 7 has nothing to do with a miraculous birth, much less one to a virgin, but with the arrival of a child who served as a sign and warning to King Ahaz. And, despite the fact that modern congregations often affirm the doctrine of the virgin birth each week when they repeat the Apostles' Creed, many twenty-first-century believers wonder if such a concept is plausible in a technological age of genetic engineering, DNA, and artificial insemination. Because this doctrine is so critical for a correct understanding of the birth stories written by both Matthew and Luke, readers should consult more extensive commentaries and Bible dictionaries and discuss the issues involved with their pastors.

A key term in any continuing discussion must necessarily be *Emmanuel* ("God with us"—a Hebrew word sometimes spelled *Immanuel*) in 1:23. For Matthew's readers it was important to understand that God was near to them in a special way in Jesus Christ. Through his birth, his preaching, and his life, death, resurrection, and ascension, Jesus was demonstrated to be the true Son of God and the anointed one ("the Messiah," see 1:1, 17; 2:4) that Jews had expected for centuries. Although the concept that God was present to believers was not new to the Jews (see Gen. 28:15; Exod. 3:1–6; Num. 23:21; Deut. 31:8; Isa. 43:5), the strong sense of the followers of Jesus that God would be as close as another human being (John 1:14) and would continue to be with them forever (1 Thess. 4:17; 2 Cor. 5: 11–17; Rev. 21:1–8) was a powerful and innovative way to reinterpret what it means to have God "with us."

The Star and the Magi (2:1–12)

In the second part of Matthew's account of Jesus' birth, modern readers encounter another well-known story. The text belies the familiar portrait we often paint of Jesus, Mary, and Joseph gathered in a stable, surrounded by angels hovering in the sky (details from Luke 2:1–20), and three magi humbly presenting their gifts. When the encounter between the magi and Jesus is described as taking place in a "house" (Matt. 2:11), it is clear that considerable time has passed since his birth and that Jesus is probably a toddler by this time. What is more, the fact that King Herod orders all boys under two years old to be murdered demonstrates that he knew that Jesus was no longer an infant (Matt. 2:16).

Although the stories of Matthew and Luke do not agree about the details of Jesus' birth, it is not necessary to try to reconcile them or dismiss one in favor of the other. Modern scholars realize that the evangelists all wrote their Gospels for different congregations, at different times, for people living in different situations, and on the basis of different sources of information. In Matthew and Luke we have two unique descriptions of the way God was made present in Jesus' life and two distinct ways in which to understand the fact that love came down at Christmas.

In Matthew's Gospel, for example, there is no stable, and there are no shepherds in the Bethlehem field. There is an angel, but his only responsibility is to inform Joseph about the nature of Jesus' unusual birth (1:20–21), and there is no singing by a heavenly choir (Luke 2:8–20). Matthew's account goes beyond the implication of a humble birth but moves into the realm of high-powered and nation-shattering politics. The magi were scholars, learned in ancient religious and philosophical texts, who were also astronomers and astrologers. Probably they came from the area northeast of Palestine ("from the East," 2:1), most likely from the Mesopotamian region around modern Iraq. Matthew says that they followed a star to the place of Jesus' birth. Scientists speculate that there may be some basis in fact for this detail, perhaps referring to an eclipse, the conjunction of planets, the explosion of a supernova, or some other astronomical event.

The description of their encounter with King Herod, a despot noted for his elaborate and creative building projects and renowned for his ruthless cruelty, indicates that the Gospel writer acknowledges that Jesus' presence overturns political expectations and can do more than bring peace on earth. Jesus' arrival may force the elite power brokers to return to the only way they know how to deal with the unknown and unexpected: with violence.[1] What happens to the two-year-olds in Bethlehem foreshadows what Jesus will endure in Jerusalem thirty or more years later.

Matthew says that the magi brought gifts to Jesus and his family. This makes sense in the context of the story, not only to help them escape the clutches of infanticide but also as signs of their desire to honor Jesus. The fact that they are not Jews but Gentiles points once more to the fact (see the discussion of the Gentile women in Jesus' family tree above, p. 10) that Jesus has come to save all the nations of the world. It is worth noting that the text does not say there were three magi. The plural term *magi* could refer to two, three, or thirty-three visitors.

Jesus: Refugee and Immigrant (2:13–18)

Once more, the messenger from God, the angel of the Lord, appears to Joseph in a dream, this time warning him of Herod's nefarious plot. There is no historical evidence that the murder of the infants actually took place in Bethlehem, but it is consistent with Herod's reputation for killing associates who crossed him, executing his wife and mother-in-law, and ordering the assassination of two of his sons at his death (an order never carried out).

Matthew sees the journey into Egypt as more than a terrible experience caused by uncontrollable circumstances. It is more than the cruel fate imposed on millions of refugees and aliens over the centuries that have been forced from their homes by oppression, war, and prejudice. It even goes beyond Jesus' solidarity with the homeless and powerless. For Matthew it is the fulfillment of the prediction from Exodus 4:22 cited in verse 15 ("Out of Egypt I have called my son") and a second Scripture in Jeremiah 31:15 (see Matt. 18) about the suffering that will precede the return of Israel to her homeland after the exile and the coming of a messiah. For Matthew and the first Christians, the son and the Messiah are both found in Jesus the Christ.

The New Exodus (2:19–23)

In the final verses of chapter 2 Matthew introduces a kind of second exodus. Just as the Jews left Palestine when Joseph's brothers fled to Egypt because of a famine (Gen. 42–49), and Israel eventually returned to the promised land after a forty-year sojourn in the desert, being led by Moses and Joshua (Exod. 12:37–40:38; Josh. 1–4), so Jesus and his parents represent the new Israel as they flee to Egypt and return after Herod dies.

Political Aspects of Matthew's Report

One important aspect of Matthew's message that is often overlooked by contemporary readers is that the Gospel not only contains a reinterpretation of the exodus and the Ten Commandments but also carries a powerful political critique of the Roman Empire. As Warren Carter points out in his perceptive study *Matthew and Empire: Initial Explorations*,[2] Matthew is more than a religious or spiritual text. It reflects a fundamental conflict between the Gospel's readers and the powerful Roman politicians and soldiers who occupied Palestine after the fall of Jerusalem in 70 CE. Matthew, as Carter points out, provides a counter-narrative to Roman political ideology and religious symbolism, using terms like *king*, *kingdom*, *power*, and *heaven*. This shows that all power does not belong to those who have large armies and financial control, but to God alone who has dominion over everything in heaven and on earth (Matt. 28:18). The account of Herod, a Roman sycophant, is just the first case in this narrative strategy. In the following chapters we will continue to point out just how important this theme is for a correct understanding of Matthew's message.

Notes

1. See Peter Richardson, *Herod, King of the Jews and Friend of the Romans* (Columbia, SC: University of South Carolina Press, 1996); and Duane W. Roller, *The Building Program of Herod the Great* (Berkeley, CA: University of California Press, 1998).
2. Warren Carter, *Matthew and Empire* (Harrisburg, PA: Trinity Press International, 2001); and *Matthew and the Margins: A Sociopolitical and Religious Reading, Initial Explorations* (Maryknoll, NY: Orbis Books, 2000).

Chapter Two

Jesus' Ministry Begins

A Study of Matthew 3:1–4:25

About Matthew's Outline

As we begin the study of the second major section of Matthew's book, it is worth considering the outline that is being followed. Although biblical scholars suggest many different possibilities, the one used here is based on literary clues that indicate a shift in Matthew's thought and presentation. Matthew 3:1 provides one obvious example: "In those days, John the Baptist appeared in the wilderness . . ." where the words "in those days" indicate a new direction in the narrative. Here are other verses where similar transitions occur:

4:23	"Jesus went throughout Galilee, teaching in their synagogues."
10:1	"Then Jesus summoned his twelve disciples."
11:1	"Now when Jesus had finished instructing his twelve disciples."
14:1	"At that time Herod the ruler heard reports about Jesus."
21:1	"When they had come near Jerusalem . . ."
28:1	"After the sabbath, as the first of the week was dawning, Mary Magdalene and the other Mary went to see the tomb."

The turning points do not hinge on historical factors or geographical directions (going from Galilee to Jerusalem, for example) but on thematic and narrative concerns. The announcement in 4:23 takes us from Jesus' call to ministry to its actual practice and what he did and taught. Matthew 10:1 indicates a change in that teaching as Jesus begins to prepare his followers for the cross, and 21:1 points to the entry into Jerusalem and Palm Sunday and the passion. Most of these verses highlight the new direction with a simple time-change reference and/or an alteration in Jesus' intentions or purpose. Matthew 28:1 introduces the climax of the whole narrative with the miraculous account of the resurrection and the formation of the church. This easily understood outline serves the purpose of helping us study the Bible from scratch. Those wishing to consider the more complex nuances of Matthew's style should consult other recent commentaries.[1]

Starting with John (3:1–17)

Having introduced the reader to Jesus' genealogy and birth account and one incident from his childhood, Matthew now fast-forwards to his adulthood and an encounter with John the Baptist. John's ministry is obviously important for understanding Jesus' identity because his story is found in all four Gospels (Mark 1:1–8; Luke 3:2–17; John 1:6–8, 19–28). Matthew presents him as one who saw himself in the line of major Old Testament prophets, especially fulfilling the prophecy from Isaiah 40:3 cited in verse 3 (also see Isa. 35:1–2, 8–10) and identifying himself with Elijah by dressing like him in the unusual garb of a coat of camel's hair and a big leather belt (v. 4; see 2 Kgs. 1:8). John was not interested in a city ministry, and by going to the wilderness he reinterprets Isaiah by making the desert the location where the forerunner of the Messiah will appear rather than a physical place that God will straighten out and level as it is described by the Old Testament writer. It is possible, as many scholars point out, that John the Baptist may have been influenced by the Essene community on the Dead Sea that withdrew to the desert to wait in purity for the messiah's coming.

John's message was one with strong spiritual connotations. Demanding that the people of Israel *repent* (change, turn around), he picks a common prophetic theme: the people have turned away from their God and must come back to their spiritual roots (see Isa. 1:27; Jer. 8:4–6; Ezek. 14:6; 18:30–31). Jesus repeats this message as a major element of his preaching, as Matthew reports in 4:17: " 'Repent, for the kingdom of heaven has come near.' "

As 3:7–10 indicates, John goes beyond the spiritual realm and introduces a powerful social component as well. He was particularly critical of the elite

Jewish religious leaders, the Pharisees and Sadducees. He was not impressed with the argument that they could trace their genealogies all the way back to Abraham, the father of the nation. For him, genetics and family trees are not the most important thing but rather what one believes and does.

The Pharisees prided themselves on their ritual purity and observance of the law and considered themselves to be expert interpreters of the Scriptures. Jesus often found himself in conflict with them, charging that they became so concerned about details and minutiae of the commandments that they missed the main point of what God was saying (see Matt. 5:20; 9:11–13; 12:2; 16:6; 23:13–16). Paul writes that he was trained as a Pharisee and that he was good at it (Phil. 3:5–6; Acts 23:6), but it took a shocking experience of meeting the resurrected Jesus (Acts 9) to change his life completely and make him realize how blind he had been.

The Sadducees, on the other hand, comprised a leadership group within Judaism founded in the second century BCE whose name meant "the righteous ones," derived from the name of a high priest, Zadok (1 Kgs. 1:26). They disagreed with the Pharisees about the nature of life and death and the role of angels, but one thing they did agree about was that they did not like Jesus' message or his ministry, and they openly consorted to have him removed from the scene (Matt. 12:14; 19:3; 16:1, 6; 22:23; also see Acts 4:1; 5:17; 23:6). The Sadducees were closely aligned with the Romans and probably feared that Jesus' revolutionary preaching would disrupt the tenuous political arrangements they had with the Roman imperial government.

John's message went beyond the notion of ritual cleansing to matters of the heart. Although the Jews had carefully developed ideas about purification and practiced acts of washing regularly (archaeologists have discovered in homes throughout Israel six-step ritual baths called *mikvaoth*), John wanted to intro-duce a cleansing by water that would not have to be repeated. It was not to be a liturgical act but an action of God that cleansed believers from the inside out. Although John baptized Jesus in the Jordan River, there is no evidence that Jesus made baptism a part of his own ministry, even though he ordered the church to practice it later (Matt. 28:19).

John's role is pivotal for Matthew (he sets the stage), and Jesus does not begin his ministry until John is arrested (4:12). In prison, however, John has his doubts and wonders if Jesus really is the one God sent (11:2–3). In a sense, the Baptist becomes one of many whose "little faith" threatens to keep them from the truth of the kingdom of heaven (see 14:31; 16:8; 17:20; 28:17). Matthew does not reveal what John finally believed as he waited to be executed. Perhaps it can be hoped that Jesus' praise was reported back to him (11:7–19), and he found, as millions of Christians have discovered, that even a little faith, when it comes to believing in Jesus, is more than enough.

Temptations and Obstacles to Ministry (4:1–11)

It is surprising that the first thing that the Spirit does for Jesus after his baptism is drive him into the wilderness and into the arms of Satan. Matthew assumes that this was according to God's purpose, possibly to toughen Jesus and get him ready for the temptations and obstacles that were yet to come. Perhaps the Tempter's propositions are ones that Jesus already had in his mind as a human being, and they now take concrete form in the dialogue that follows. Maybe the temptations were ongoing, and Jesus had to struggle with them throughout his life. As Luke 4:13 puts it, "When the devil had finished every test, he departed from him until an opportune time."

Matthew reports that there were three obstacles thrown up to Jesus. Mark says nothing about them and limits his description to a mere two verses (Mark 1:12–13). John's Gospel does not mention the incident at all. In Matthew's version, the first temptation comes because Jesus has been fasting in the desert forty days and forty nights. The number forty is significant because it bears scriptural symbolism. Noah's flood lasted forty days (Gen. 7:4, 12, 17); Moses fasted for the same amount of time (Exod. 24:18); and the Jews were in the wilderness during the exodus for forty years (Exod. 16:35). Jesus himself will appear to the disciples forty days after his resurrection (Acts 1:3).

In this case, the Tempter urges Jesus to turn bread into stone, presumably to feed himself. But more was involved. Throughout his ministry Jesus was concerned about feeding hungry and starving people (see Matt. 5:6; for the feeding of the multitudes, see 14:13–21; 15:32–38). The round rocks in the desert looked like loaves of bread, and if Jesus could have the power to produce food in abundance, he could feed God's people all over the world. But Jesus resists the offer. Quoting Deuteronomy 8:3 he makes it clear that he must do what God wants him to do. He has come to feed not only those who lack food but also those who are spiritually hungry. It will be up to those who follow him to fill the world's food banks and hospitality centers (25:31–46).

The second temptation is equally enticing. Taking Jesus on a virtual tour of Jerusalem, the Tempter shows him the highest point of the Temple near the Western Wall. This time it is Satan who quotes Scripture, reminding Jesus that Psalm 91:11–12 promises that those who are favored by God will be borne up by angels. But Jesus is not impressed with this kind of biblical knowledge and corrects Satan's interpretation by citing an alternative verse from Deuteronomy 6:16: "Do not put the LORD your God to the test." Jesus has to depend on God and not create a popularized ministry that uses fantastic tricks or elements of entertainment to energize his message, no matter how spectacular they are. He is not about to become a circus performer or a magician to get people to listen. As Hebrews puts it, "Because he himself was tested by what he suffered, he is able to help those who are being tested" (Heb. 2:18).

In the final challenge the Tempter takes Jesus to the political and military heights to show him what he will be able to accomplish if he worships evil. If Jesus cuts a deal with the devil, he will be able to have tremendous power without limits. The kingdoms of the world will be his, and he will be able to achieve great things, possibly even good things. All he has to do is be willing to compromise the high standards of God. Here Jesus comes face to face with the temptation of using evil to accomplish good, being willing to sacrifice a few to help the many, using political structures to do God's work. Here he has to choose which empire he will serve and foster. Will it be an empire that takes on the imperium of Rome and the worldwide influence of the emperor? Will he form a revolutionary group that fights for world domination? Or will he acknowledge that God is the only real king? Citing part of Deuteronomy 6:12–14, he remembers the words of Israel's first great leader, Moses, and how he told the people to keep their priorities straight.

After the Tempter gives up (at least temporarily) and leaves him, and the angels of God minister to him, Jesus makes it clear in Matthew 4:17 that the empire he is committed to is not one of secular power and military might but one he calls "the empire (or kingdom) of heaven." As Warren Carter puts it, "Jesus' actions, guided by the scriptures and vindicated by ministering angels, focus on God's will, resist the devil, and advocate an alternate existence constituted by God's purposes."[2]

Teaching and Healing in Galilee (4:12–25)

Jesus begins his ministry in Galilee, the northern end of Palestine, south of modern Lebanon and west of Syria. According to Matthew, Jesus was raised in this area, in the small city of Nazareth (2:23), and later settled in the fishing village of Capernaum (4:13) as an adult. Much of his preaching and teaching took place around the Sea of Galilee, also known as the Sea of Chinnereth (named after a harp, an instrument its shape suggests; see Num. 34:11; Josh. 12:3; 13:27), and later called the Sea of Tiberias (John 6:1; 21:1). Luke more accurately refers to it as a "lake" (Luke 5:1, 2; 8:22–23, 33). The main north-south road known as the *Via Maris* followed part of its western shoreline through Capernaum (a Roman road marker is still visible there) and helped that area develop as a fishing and agricultural center.

Jesus' adult hometown of Capernaum was really named *Kefer Naum* in Hebrew, which means "village of Naum," or perhaps it would be called Naum Town today. It was a major fishing village where Peter and his family lived and, according to Luke's Gospel, was the place where a Roman official built a synagogue in honor of Jesus' healing of his slave (Luke 7:2, 5). It is currently a national archaeological site in Israel where the black basalt foundation of the first century CE synagogue that Jesus preached in (John 6:59) can still be seen. It is also the location of a later Byzantine church built on the traditional site of Peter's house. The Franciscans constructed a modern octagonal Christian sanctuary there in 1990.

Matthew 4:18–22 records the call of the first disciples. Jesus begins to build his ministerial staff by inviting the brothers Peter and Andrew to follow him. Since they were part of the Capernaum fishing industry, he urges them to change their vocation in order to "fish for people" (v. 19). Possibly he has Jeremiah 16:16 in mind, where God promises to raise leaders to bring Israel back from exile: "I am now sending for many fishermen, says the LORD, and they shall catch them."

A second group of brothers, James and John, leave their father's business and also join them. The fact that they leave *immediately* indicates how powerful and compelling Jesus' call to ministry is. They do not even take time to settle their affairs or say goodbye to loved ones.

The section ends with a summary statement of Jesus' teaching and mission activities. It is a review of what he normally said and did, that is, preach the *good news* (gospel) of the coming of the kingdom of heaven and heal the sick. Mark reports that the disciples, in addition to being called to be with him, were also empowered to carry on these same ministries in his name (Mark 3:13–19). Jesus' healing activities are reported in detail throughout Matthew's book and are indications that he is indeed God's Messiah. As the prophets foretold, when the Messiah comes he will bring the spirit of wisdom and understanding (Isa. 11:2), the eyes of the blind will be opened, the deaf will be made to hear (Isa. 35:5–7).

Notes

1. Ulrich Luz, for example, in his three-volume commentary, breaks the book into six major sections with seventeen subsections (see *Matthew 1–7*, Hermenia [Minneapolis: Fortress Press, 2007]; *Matthew 8–20*, Hermenia [Minneapolis: Fortress Press, 2001]; and *Matthew 21–28*, Hermenia [Minneapolis: Fortress Press, 2005]). In his two-volume commentary, Donald Hagner (*Matthew 1–13,* Word Biblical Commentary, vol. 33A [Dallas: Word Books, 1993]; and *Matthew 14–28,* Word Biblical Commentary, vol. 33B [Dallas: Word Books, 1995]) divides it into sixteen divisions. Warren Carter, in *Matthew and the Margins: A Sociopolitical and Religious Reading, Initial Explorations* (Maryknoll, NY: Orbis Books, 2000) identifies six critical narrative blocks with twenty-seven subdivisions.
2. Carter, *Matthew and the Margins*, 107.

Chapter Three

The Core of Jesus' Teaching and Healing

A Study of Matthew 5:1–9:38

The Sermon on the Mount: The Charter of Human Freedom
(Chaps. 5–7)

From the first days of the Christian church, the Sermon on the Mount has provided believers with guidelines to live more God-centered lives in the spirit of Christ. Already in the book of James there appear to be references to the sermon (Jas. 2:10, 13; 5:2, 10–12), and Clement, the first bishop of Rome (died around 96 CE), quotes it directly in his letters (*1 Clem.* 13:1–2; *2 Clem.* 4:2; 6:1; 13:4). It is also cited frequently in the *Didache, or Teaching of the Twelve Apostles* (written around 100 CE), an instructional handbook for new disciples.

Sometimes called "the original charter of human freedom,"[1] "the essence of the Christian faith and life,"[2] or "the quintessence of the teaching of Jesus,"[3] the poignant instructions in Matthew 5–7 and Luke 6 (often called "the Sermon on the Plain") clearly have had a powerful influence on the church ever since.

The Sermon on the Mount also provides universal religious appeal. It has played a role in the development of Islam and modern Judaism, and Mahatma Gandhi said that if he only had to face the words of Jesus there and his interpretation of them, even he could admit to being a Christian.[4] "It goes straight to the heart," as Gandhi put it.[5]

The Location of the Mount (5:1)

Matthew makes it clear at the beginning and end of chapters 5–7 that he wants to locate the place of Jesus' teaching on a mountain (5:1; 7:28–8:1). By identifying the setting so carefully (although he does not say which mountain) he helps his readers connect Jesus' teaching to the Ten Commandments given to Moses on a mountain in the wilderness of Sinai (Exod. 19:3, 12; 24:12–18; 34:1–4). A mountain, to which God descends in a cloud to speak to Moses, is also prominent in the account of Jesus' transfiguration (17:1) when the divine voice declares that Jesus truly is the beloved Son. At the end of the Gospel, Jesus appears for a final time on the heights to send his disciples on a worldwide mission (28:16). For Matthew, Jesus presents a new interpretation of the Ten Commandments and appears as the new Moses who will lead God's people. In Luke's version, the mountain is where the twelve disciples are called to service whereas the teaching is given below "on a level place" (Luke 6:17).

Traditionally, Christians have identified the place where Jesus preached the Sermon on the Mount with Tabgha (also called Heptapegon), on the western side of the Sea of Galilee about seven miles north of the modern city of Tiberius, just south of Jesus' hometown of Capernaum. It is really not a mountain but a natural amphitheater scooped out of a hillside, and it is also considered the location for the enactment of the miracle of the loaves and fishes (Matt. 14:13–21). It is unlikely that Matthew 5–7 actually constitutes a single sermon; it is more likely a collection of the things that Jesus regularly taught, assembled and edited by Matthew. Today the Chapel of the Beatitudes (built in 1937–1938) marks the area where a fourth-century-CE church was built to honor Jesus' teaching. A small pavilion down by the lake provides a wonderful spot for pilgrims to pray or celebrate the Lord's Supper together as they try to visualize the places where Jesus worked and lived.

A Sampling of Key Passages in Chapter 5

The commentator Ulrich Luz captures the critical nature of chapters 5–7 when he writes, "The Sermon on the Mount is the first extensive proclamation of Jesus in the Gospel of Matthew. For that reason alone it has a foundational character. It is the only discourse of Jesus that almost exclusively contains commandments of Jesus."[6] Modern readers may be familiar with the central passages, such as the Beatitudes (5:1–11), the Lord's Prayer (6:5–15), the so–called "Golden Rule" (7:7–12), the difficult teaching about loving one's enemies (5:38–42; 7:1–6), and the foolishness of being anxious about money (6:19–34). In a short study like this one it is impossible, of course, to give adequate attention to the depths of Jesus' instruction. Although the Sermon on the Mount provides the core of his spirituality and the definition of his theology of ministry, we must be content here to highlight a few of his key teachings.[7]

The Beatitudes (5:1–11)

The Sermon on the Mount begins with one of the best-known passages in the whole Bible (5:1–11). The word "beatitude" refers to the fact that Jesus' teaching is based on a form of instruction, which traditionally includes information about God's blessing of the faithful. The main concept is that if disciples act in certain ways, God will bless them. This kind of teaching is visible in the Old Testament, in Psalm 1, for example, correctly translated in the Revised Standard Version of the Bible as " 'Blessed is the man [*sic*] who walks not in the counsel of the wicked, nor stands in the way of sinners.' " The more modern version found in the New Revised Standard Version (and other translations), " 'Happy are those who do not follow the advice of the wicked,' " is misleading because even a quick glance at the Beatitudes demonstrates that there is nothing happy or emotionally uplifting about being spiritually poor, mourning, hungering for truth, or working for peace in a violent world. Referring to them as "the Behappytudes" is not helpful. The point that is really being made is not about psychological contentment but about the need for one to find power and strength in God, to be socially involved, and to find the blessing that only comes through God's presence in tough times.

It is worthwhile to look at one of the Beatitudes in a little detail since many of them are easily misunderstood. In the case of the third beatitude, " 'Blessed are the meek,' " for example, it is often incorrectly thought that meekness here refers to a mild, dispassionate, weak kind of approach to conflict that causes Christians to be run over and despised. In fact, the word "meek" (Gk., *praeis*) refers to a person or a wild animal that is "tamed," not submissive. A better translation today might be " 'Blessed are those who are tamed by the Spirit, for they will inherit the earth.' " Paul uses a similar word in Galatians 5:23 when he lists "gentleness" (*prautus*) as a fruit of the Holy Spirit. The same idea is found in Matthew 11:29–30 where Jesus speaks about the training of a huge ox for work in a farmer's field: " 'Take my yoke upon you, and learn from me; for I am gentle [Gr., *praus*] and humble in heart, and you will find rest for your souls. For my yoke is easy, and my burden is light' " (also see Gal. 6:1; Eph. 4:2; Titus 3:2; 1 Pet. 3:16).

Reinterpreting the Ten Commandments (5:17–37)

Another section worth examining is 5:17–37. Here Jesus discusses the Ten Commandments and the Torah and offers fresh insights into their true significance. Throughout Matthew's Gospel Jesus is concerned that his opponents are so determined to keep the letter of the law that they miss its spiritual intent. In 5:17–20 he indicates that he knows that the law is good and warns against rationalizing its intention to enable believers to duck some of its harsher demands. The next passage (5:21–26) reinterprets the concept of murder. Killing someone is more than taking physical life away; it also involves the emotional and psychological acts to slander and hurt another person. A similar conclusion is reached about the seventh commandment (5:27–32). Adultery is more than a sexual act. It involves lust and hidden sexual desire. In 5:33–37 he returns to the commandment that forbids taking the Lord's name in vain in an oath (Exod. 20:7). Since it was common for people to swear on all kinds of things to establish (or pretend to establish) the truth, Jesus contends that the truth should be able to stand on its own. If one is honest, "Yes" and "No" are more than enough.

A key concept is found in Jesus' repetition of the expression " 'You have heard it said of old,' " followed by " 'but I say unto you' " (see 5:21, 27, 33, 38, 43). Jesus is not content with the old rationalizations. The new empire of God requires a renewed understanding of the real intent of God's law.

The reader who wishes to have a clear understanding of the sayings in chapters 6 and 7 (including the Lord's Prayer) can easily see why additional study is needed.

The Beginning of the Healing Mission (8:1–9:38)

This section continues Jesus' instruction given to the disciples and the people, this time through the agency of miracles rather than sermons or dialogue. Matthew 8:1 sets the stage as it points to a change in venue when Jesus comes down from the mountain and a large crowd follows. The main function of chapters 8 and 9 is summarized in 9:35–38. Jesus abandons the strategy of speaking in one place and now moves freely throughout the cities and villages, teaching in synagogues (as he already has before, 4:15–17, 23).

Although Matthew says in chapters 8 and 9 that Jesus' purpose in these journeys is to proclaim the gospel (9:35), no examples of his teaching or sermons are recounted. Presumably Matthew and his readers know that the miracle stories are included not merely to provide a medical handbook for future Christian healers—they also offer important lessons about the meaning of discipleship and Christian mission:

- What it means to interact with those who are shunned by society as unclean (the lepers, 8:1–4)

- The fact that even Roman officers can have great faith, perhaps even more than that exhibited by Israel's elite and privileged religious leaders (8:10–13)

- How Jesus came not only to heal physical infirmities but also, as the quotation from Isaiah's Suffering Servant passage (Isa. 53:4–5) demonstrates, to forgive sin (see the story of the healing of the paralytic in 9:1–7)

Other lessons are equally impressive and important. Serving Jesus has to be an absolute priority. Even observing elaborate rituals to honor the dead, mourning for twelve months or more (8:21–22), must be abandoned in order to get on with the urgent work of the kingdom.

The story of the harnessing of the storm on the lake (8:23–27), demonstrates, furthermore, that even those who are most committed to Jesus may be handicapped by a severe lack of confidence and faith. When they discover that even nature takes orders from Jesus (compare with 8:8), they are totally amazed. He is not a run-of-the-mill faith healer. As Psalm 65:7 puts it, God's power is awesome: "You silence the roaring of the seas, the roaring of their waves, the tumult of the peoples" (see also Pss. 89:9; 107:29).

In the final miracle of this section (9:27–34) Matthew describes the healing of the blind and mute. The importance of faith is emphasized here when the (two) blind men acknowledge that they believe that Jesus has the ability to heal them. That he is able to cast out demons amazes the onlookers because they know he could only do this if he had the power of God with him. Matthew also wants his readers to think about the well-known prophecy in Isaiah 35:5–7 that predicts that when the messiah comes he will have the ability to open the eyes of the blind and unstop the ears of the deaf. That Jesus can do this clearly shows who he is.

The healing of blindness, in fact, becomes a key feature of Jesus' healing ministry, and Matthew indicates that more than a physical malady is of concern: spiritual myopia is also a critical illness that only can be healed through contact with the Messiah. Two blind men follow Jesus when they regain their sight (20:34), and Jesus reserves his harshest criticism for the Pharisees, whom he calls "blind fools" (23:17) and "blind guides" (23:24; also see 23:26; John 9). These religious leaders put on an impressive display but are corrupt from the inside out.

Insertions in the Healing Account (9:9–13; 9:14–17; 9:35–38)

In the midst of his account of Jesus' healing mission, Matthew inserts three passages that set the stage for his second round of teaching and the training of the disciples in chapters 10–13. In 9:9–13 and 9:14–17, for example, he interrupts the flow of the narrative when he inserts two passages about discipleship, and he completes this section with a comment about the need for additional workers on the mission field (9:35–38).

The first two passages are difficult to interpret. Although the person Jesus calls into discipleship is named Matthew in 9:9–13, in parallel texts in Mark 2:13–17 and Luke 5:27–32 he is called Levi. Are the two men the same person, or has Matthew changed the disciple's name for his own purposes? Whatever happened, it is clear that Matthew (or a later editor) wants to call attention to the fact that Matthew has a special place in the list of disciples. With the insertion of this account just before the twelve are sent out on mission (10:1–13) Matthew is given prominence. Matthew's text may help explain why the later church thought that the apostle Matthew wrote the first Gospel. In these verses they may sense that the author is calling attention to his own primary relationship to Jesus.

At the end of this section in 9:32–34 Matthew points to an ominous shadow that this central feature of Jesus' ministry is casting. Already the Pharisees are trying to create doubt about who he really is and are setting the stage for confrontation with him and the crucifixion. " 'By the ruler of the demons,' " they snarl, " 'he casts out demons.' "

All of this shows, even the negative aspects, that God is at work in Jesus' miracles and teachings. Regardless of what the religious leaders think, the people as a whole respond positively to his ministry (9:35–36). Considering the innovation and vitality of Jesus' message it is clear that even more workers (" 'laborers' ") are needed: " 'The harvest is plentiful, but the laborers are few; therefore ask the Lord of the harvest to send out laborers into his harvest' " (9:37–38).

Notes

1. E. Stanley Jones, *The Christ of the Mount* (Nashville: Abingdon Press, 1931, 1958), 21.
2. William Barclay, *The Beatitudes and the Lord's Prayer for Everyman* (New York: Harper & Row, 1964), 11.
3. Hans Dieter Betz, *The Sermon on the Mount* (Minneapolis: Fortress Press, 1995), 3.
4. Louis Fischer, *Gandhi, His Life and Message for the World* (New York: New American Library, 1954), 131.
5. William L. Shirer, *Gandhi, a Memoir* (New York: Simon & Schuster, 1979), 95.
6. Ulrich Luz, *Matthew 1–7*, Hermenia (Minneapolis: Fortress Press, 2007), 176.
7. Luz, *Matthew 1–7*, for example, devotes 230 pages to Matt. 5–7 whereas Betz's master commentary in the Hermenia series runs 714 pages!

Chapter Four

Expanded Urban Mission

A Study of Matthew 10:1–13:58

The opening verse of this long section of Matthew's narrative is closely connected to 9:35–38. Together they summarize the account of the calling of the disciples that Matthew found in Mark 3:13–19. The followers of Jesus were given three specific tasks: to teach the good news, heal the sick, and be with him. In these chapters emphasis is primarily on instruction of the disciples and the assembled people, with a powerful denouement in chapter 13 where the process of teaching and preaching is encapsulated: some will hear and learn, and some will not; some will see, and some will shut their eyes.

The Role of the Disciples (10:1–11)

In the first chapter of Matthew's fourth section (chap. 10) Jesus focuses on preparing the disciples for their special ministry with him. In 11:1 that instruction ends for a time, and they move out in urban mission.

Matthew 10:1–4 provides the list of the twelve apostles, whose names are also found in Mark 6:7–13 and Luke 9:1–16. Those who will be particularly prominent in later stories include Peter, the spokesman for the whole group; his brother Andrew; James and John; and Judas. Ironically, from the beginning Judas is depicted in a bad light. He never is seen as a positive force. Judas is a traitor, the Benedict Arnold of the group right from the first: "the one who betrayed him" (v. 4).

The next few verses (10:5–15) provide the modus operandi for the new apostles. They are given the title "apostles" even though it is probably not one that Jesus used himself. Matthew employs this term because it was an important designation used later in the early church to identify the first authentic followers of Jesus. See Paul's discussion of the importance of this title in Galatians 1:1–18.

In Matthew's Gospel the work of mission is primarily designed to reach the Jewish people, not the non-Jews in Palestine and other countries who are defined by the pejorative term "Gentiles." The disciples are not to teach outsiders or enter the towns of the Samaritans, traditional enemies of the Jews. Their mission is to "the lost sheep of Israel."

The message they bring is that which Jesus proclaimed earlier in Matthew 4:17: " 'The kingdom of heaven has come near.' " In addition to preaching, the disciples are also to engage in a healing ministry and exercise their ministry without payment. As a strictly nonprofit organization, the disciples are to depend exclusively on God's provision: they can take no money, extra clothes, or credit cards. They are God's messengers, and the people who receive ministry should provide for them as laborers worthy of their hire (10:10).

Danger and Encouragement (10:12–23; 11:1–10)

In this section, Matthew indicates that the followers of Jesus can expect to be put in harm's way. Right from the start, Jesus tells the disciples that some cities and towns will reject them. They can test the situation out by the way in which their message is received (10:14). If people do not welcome them, they must understand that some listeners are so spiritually blind that they will be hostile to the good news of God. In such cases the disciples should forget about them and with a gesture of contempt, shake the dust of the place from off their feet (10:14). Compare the action of the prophet Nehemiah when the people refused to listen to him: "I also shook out the fold of my garment and said, 'So may God shake out everyone from house and from property who does not perform this promise. Thus may they be shaken out and emptied' " (Neh. 5:13).

Similarly in Matthew 10:16–23 the disciples are warned in graphic terms about the dangers that lie ahead. Reflecting the kind of persecution that early Christians actually experienced later at the hands of Jewish opponents or Roman prosecutors, believers are warned to expect family opposition as well as official proceedings. Although it will be extremely difficult, they are assured of God's powerful support: " 'The one who endures to the end will be saved' " (v. 22). Paul's writings demonstrate the humiliations, beatings, "insults, hardships, persecutions, and calamities" (2 Cor. 12:10) that he experienced before his official trial in Rome (see Acts 21–28; 2 Cor. 12:10; 2 Cor. 11:16–12:9) and later New Testament books outline the suffering that Jesus' followers did encounter later (see Hebrews, 1 and 2 Peter, and Jude).

Jesus assures the disciples in 10:24–33 that they truly can make it through the hardships of ministry. Since " 'a disciple is not above the teacher' " (v. 24), they can be comforted that Jesus has already been through the same sufferings that they can expect. As Hebrews 2:18 puts it, "Because he himself was tested by what he suffered, he is able to help those who are being tested." The truth must be boldly proclaimed in public, and they should not even fear the prospect of death. Regardless of what enemies do to them, their souls (v. 28), the inner spiritual center that defines who they really are, will survive. At the last judgment (vv. 32–33) Jesus will be their advocate and support those who have acknowledged him in this life. As already noted in chapter 2 (pp. 16–17), the accounts of John the Baptist's last days (11:2–19; 14:1–12) provide additional illustrations of the kind of suffering followers of Jesus may be forced to endure. His story illustrates what Jesus meant when he encouraged the disciples in 10:19, " 'When they hand you over, do not worry about how you are to speak or what you are to say; for what you are to say will be given to you at that time.' " John's doubt demonstrates that even the strongest believers may sometimes be tested, almost beyond endurance.

Jesus' sharp criticism of two places he knew well (11:20–24), the lakeside cities of Chorazin and Bethsaida, indicates that even people who knew Jesus on a day-to-day basis could misunderstand him and turn on him. Jesus says that their behavior was worse than that found in the Gentile cities of Tyre and Sidon. In Capernaum, the town he chose for his hometown, the situation was so bad that it could only be compared to the sinfulness of Old Testament cities of Sodom and Gomorrah, places so notorious for their immoral behavior and rejection of God that they were destroyed (Gen. 19:24; Isa. 1:9; Matt. 10:15; Jude 6). (For a discussion of Jesus' saying (11:26–30) about being weary and carrying heavy burdens see chap. 3 above [p. 23].)

Mounting Religious Opposition (12:1–50)

Chapter 12 provides details about the hostility Jesus experienced at the hands of the leading religious leaders in Palestine (already hinted at in 9:34). The story about grabbing a snack of grain on the day of Sabbath rest (Friday night through Saturday afternoon) involves a matter of interpretation of Old Testament Scripture. The Pharisees were convinced that strict kosher rules must be observed about eating, drinking, and walking to preserve the fourth commandment, which prohibited working on the Sabbath: "You shall not do any work—you, your son or your daughter, your male or female slave, your livestock, or the alien resident in your towns" (Exod. 20:10). Jesus indicates how ridiculous such laws can be when people are hungry. Citing the example of David, the founder of the kingdom of Israel, he showed how people of faith can be flexible in using their common sense for interpreting religious rules by citing the example where the priest gave soldiers holy bread when they were in need (1 Sam. 21:1–6). This incident, he says, took place in God's temple; but in him they find something greater than any building. Calling himself " 'the Son of Man,' " he indicates that he is the lord and master of Sabbath rules (12:8) and is free to give them new meaning.

A similar example follows in 12:9–14 when Jesus heals a man with an injured hand on the Sabbath. Again, the Pharisees criticize Jesus for working on the Sabbath. Although he points out that it is better to help someone, even on the Sabbath, than to stand by idly and do nothing, the Pharisees are so infuriated they begin their plan to kill him (12:14). In 12:22–37 they mount the most severe attack to date, accusing him of being in league with Beelzebul, the mythical "Lord of the Flies," the ruler of all demons. Here Jesus points out the irrationality of their argument. How could someone who is the chief demon be responsible for casting out his own cohorts, as he and the disciples regularly do? How could a strong man defeat a powerful force like Satan without first subduing and binding him? If Jesus can defeat Satan, then it must be clear that he is not working with evil. In fact, the opposite is true: " 'If it is by the Spirit of God that I cast out demons, then the kingdom of God has come to you' " (12:28).

The passage about opposing evil and good and the following comment about blasphemy in 12:30–32 are sources of much confusion and consternation to many modern Christian readers. In response to the Pharisees' claim that Jesus is in league with Satan, Jesus says gravely that " 'people will be forgiven for every sin and blasphemy, but blasphemy against the Holy Spirit will not be forgiven. Whoever speaks a word against the Son of Man will be forgiven, but whoever speaks against the Spirit will not be forgiven, either in this age or the age to come.' " Often this warning is misunderstood, and readers today worry that there must be ways that they can inadvertently offend the Holy Spirit and be eternally condemned. But 12:22–37 shows the context in which this saying must be correctly interpreted. In these verses Jesus makes it clear that his opponents are deliberately distorting the truth. They do not simply misunderstand his mission. They want to twist the facts and make his good work appear to be evil. Since the Holy Spirit is the one who has empowered him (Matt. 4:1–11), such fabrication is also an attack on the Spirit. Those who do this kind of thing do not do so unintentionally. On purpose they are trying to make God's goodness appear to be devilish, and in such a way they condemn themselves.

In 12:38–45 the scribes and Pharisees continue their attack. Their request in verse 38 for a sign, some kind of visible evidence, like a miracle, that would confirm that Jesus is really from God, seems innocent enough superficially. Is it not true that the Messiah will perform signs and wonders? But Jesus rejects such a demand as unbelief. Citing the Old Testament story of Jonah, he refers to the one miracle that really establishes his identity. As Jonah was rescued after being in the belly of the "sea-monster" (not a whale, as people often assume) for three days and nights, so Jesus, as one greater than Jonah, will be raised from the dead after three days. The resurrection will be the true sign that will prove who Jesus is, not the performance of on-demand miracles requested by those who are trying to discredit his power.

In the final passage in this section (12:46–50), Matthew builds on verses found in Mark 3:20–34. There Mark hints that even Jesus' mother and brothers had their doubts about his true identity, because in addition to the Pharisees accusing him of being in league with the unclean spirits, his family members declare, " 'He has gone out of his mind' " (Mark 3:21). Matthew apparently finds the idea that Jesus' family members could be grossly mistaken about him repugnant and eliminates this accusation. By the time Matthew wrote his Gospel, Jesus' family members were probably already church leaders (see the comments about his brother James in Acts 12:17; 15:13–21; 1 Cor. 15:7; Gal. 1:19; 2:9, 12), and his mother was so highly respected that it may have seemed inappropriate to cast a shadow on her memory or the position of his brothers in the early church.

How the Word Is Spread (13:1–11)

As already indicated at the beginning of this chapter, the parable of the Sower provides a powerful conclusion to this whole section of Matthew's report about Jesus' instruction of the disciples. In fact, all three of the Synoptic Gospels give Jesus' teaching and the parable of the Sower special prominence and report it in similar detail (Mark 4:1–9; Luke 8:4–8). Mark says that if the disciples do not understand this parable, they will not understand any of the others because the parable of the Sower defines what preaching and understanding are really all about (Mark 4:13).

In all three Synoptic Gospels the parable of the Sower reflects the area in which Jesus grew up and ministered to, for it is a story from everyday life. The story is about farming, about how the same seeds give different yields depending on the kind of soil they fall on, so it is one that all of his hearers would be able to understand. For Matthew, the implications for teachers and preachers are clear. Preaching is like sowing seed and growing grain. Growth, whether in agriculture or on the mission field, is not always dependent on the skill of the ones sowing the seeds. The soil and the listeners are also responsible, and often their inner nature and dispositions to receive the seed are determinative: " 'Let anyone with ears listen!' " (v. 9).

Jesus in the Boat (13:2)

It is worth noting in 13:2 that the comment "[Jesus] got into a boat and sat there, while the whole crowd stood on the beach" is not an insignificant detail. Recently it has received new importance through an amazing archaeological discovery. In 1986, during a drought in the area of the Sea of Galilee, a boat that had sunk during the first century CE was discovered in the mud at Kinneret, south of the city of Tiberius. After it was carefully preserved and moved to a museum built nearby to house it, it was chemically treated for several years and is now available to public viewing. "The Jesus boat," as it is often called, was two-masted with a length of about twenty-seven feet and beam of about seven feet seven inches and could have easily held twelve fishermen and a preacher. While such artifacts do not scientifically prove the veracity of the Gospel stories, they provide interesting data that make them real to believers of any age. When visitors see the Kinneret boat in person or view the many videos of it available on the Internet, they realize that Jesus and the disciples were not recluses operating out of isolated circumstances but that they preached and provided ministry in real places that can still be seen today.

The Interpretation (13:18–23)

The parable of the Sower that Jesus delivered from such a boat is also important for another reason: it is one of two stories of Jesus for which he provided an extended explanation (the other is the parable of the Weeds, Matt. 13:36–43). In Matthew 13:10–17, the disciples and Jesus have an interactive session in which questions are put to him about his method of teaching in parables. Parables are often defined as stories with symbolic meanings and were frequently used by Jesus to teach about the kingdom of heaven.[1]

Matthew 13:18–23 is usually called "the interpretation of the parable of the Sower" because in these verses Jesus provides an explanation of the story previously told. Most scholars, while acknowledging that the parable of the Sower certainly can be traced back to Jesus himself, also recognize that the interpretation found in three different forms in the Gospels of Matthew, Mark, and Luke (Mark 4:13–20; Luke 8:11–15) most likely reflects the understandings of the parable developed by the early church as they struggled much later with its meaning. The language used in all three Gospels is more typical of later situations than the time of Jesus, and the fact that the interpretations treat the parable as an allegory, in which every detail must be interpreted symbolically, goes beyond the simplicity that generally characterized his teaching style.

The fact that the Gospel writers were comfortable in applying their own interpretations of the parable of the Sower to Jesus' parable is instructive. It demonstrates that they believed that Jesus' words could be reinterpreted for new situations and new times and that the church had the right and obligation to make them fresh and new.

Matthew's version of the interpretation (13:18–23) emphasizes the fact that simply hearing the "the words of the kingdom" is not enough. In his church some people must have been so resistant to Jesus' teaching that it seemed as if some outside forces were preventing them from being understood. As Matthew says, some misunderstood because of the evil one. Others were deterred by political pressure, concern about public opinion, and official persecution. As Warren Carter puts it, "The person does not understand that God's empire confronts, threatens, and conflicts with cultural values and structures, and that 'the empire' strikes back."[2] Only those who truly listen and hear, "the good soil," finally bear fruit for God's work.

Additional Parables from Daily Life (13:24–53)

In the rest of Matthew 13 seven more parables are provided that strengthen and expand the initial parable of the Sower. All of them are from incidents in first-century-CE village life dealing with farming, household chores, buying or selling, and the fishing industry. As we have already pointed out, although Matthew found the parable of the Sower and the parable of the Mustard Seed in Mark's text, he adds one that he has in common with Luke (parable of the Yeast—although Luke 13:20–21 has it in a different context), and four that are only found in his Gospel (presumably from his special source called "M"). The flexibility with which the three evangelists constructed their parable chapters is also demonstrated by the fact that Mark has an additional story that is only found in his Gospel (parable of the Growing Seed, Mark 4:26–29), whereas Luke limits his presentation entirely to the parable of the Sower and its interpretation. It is evident perhaps that in order to understand Matthew's intentions fully, it is as necessary to see what he leaves out as it is to observe what he puts in.

Another Rejection (13:54–58)

Matthew concludes this section of his book as he did the last section in 9:32–34. Jesus is in real danger, and his opponents do not believe that he has come from

God: "Who does he think he is?" they argue. " 'His father is just a common car-penter, and we know his mother Mary. His brothers are no better than any of us, and we know their names: James, Joseph [named after his father], Judas [ironic that Jesus had a brother with the same name as his betrayer], and Simon [the same name two of the disciples had; see 10:2–4]" (13:54–58, paraphr.). As Jesus and the disciples continue to travel throughout Palestine, more and more people hear about him, and as he draws closer to Jerusalem, the opposition ominously begins to include government and religious officials at a much higher level.[3]

Matthew's Portrayal of the Disciples in Contrast to Mark's

In Matthew 13 one major difference between the presentations of Matthew and Mark is seen in their contrasting views of the disciples. In Mark's Gospel the disciples, even though they choose to follow Jesus, remain spiritually blind and are not really sure who Jesus is. In some ways, the warning quoted from Isaiah 6 in Mark 4:12 applies as much to them as it does to the people who reject Jesus' teaching altogether: "They will indeed look, but not perceive." They do not understand the central parable of the Sower (Mark 4:13); they are afraid when Jesus stills the storm (4:35–41); they fail to understand the significance of his ability to feed the masses (8:14–21); they misinterpret Jesus' assertion that he is the Christ (8:27–9:1); and at the end they all deny him and run away from the cross.

In Matthew's account, however, it is clear that the author does not want to depict the followers of Jesus in such a negative light. According to Matthew, it is his disciples that really understand him and can be considered his true fam-ily (Matt. 12:48–49). They are the ones who have been given the secrets of the kingdom of heaven and have blessed ears and eyes (13:16–17). Peter is given the keys to the kingdom (16:19), and at the end of the Gospel the disciples receive Jesus' authority to bring the church to the world (28:16–20). In Mark's account, on the other hand, the women run away in fear, and the story ends with-out an appearance of the risen Lord and with an enigmatic closing comment: "They said nothing to anyone, for they were afraid" (Mark 16:8).

In passages like this the editorial work of each Gospel writer is evident. Matthew and Mark write at different times in the church's history. They are trying to communicate to different sets of readers, so they see the story of Jesus from divergent perspectives. In the case of the blindness of the disciples (Mark) or their special enlightenment (Matthew), modern readers need further study to understand the overall purposes of various accounts of Jesus' ministry in the Gospels and how the writers adjust them to bring the good news, each in his own special way. In Matthew's Gospel the disciples are not forced to search for Jesus' true identity after the resurrection. Before his report ends, they already understand who he is and are poised to bring the good news to the rest of the world (Matt. 28:16–20).

Notes

1. For some other examples in Matthew see 4:31, 32; 20:1–15; 21:33–42; 22:1–14; 25:1–12. To see how this has been carried out in the Reformed tradition, see my book *Witness Without Parallel: Eight Biblical Texts That Make Us Presbyterian* (Louisville, KY: Geneva Press, 2003).
2. Warren Carter, *Matthew and the Margins: A Sociopolitical and Religious Reading, Initial Explorations* (Maryknoll, NY: Orbis Books, 2000), 286.
3. For the background of the Jewish groups that opposed Jesus see Richard A. Horsley, *Scribes, Visionaries, and the Politics of Second Temple Judea* (Louisville, KY: Westminster John Knox Press, 2007).

Chapter Five

Prelude to Jerusalem

A Study of Matthew 14:1–20:34

This section of Matthew is not only the longest in our study but also the most extended one in the Gospel—with good reason. In the NRSV Jesus' preparation for his passion, the description of Palm Sunday, the week before the crucifixion, and the resurrection and ascension take up about 53 percent of Matthew's text.

As Raymond Brown points out, the Gospels were written backward. In the first days of the church, believers were primarily interested in the resurrection and ascension of Jesus and communicating the new life in Christ to a skeptical world. Thus in Paul's writings the resurrection is the central doctrine of the good news (1 Cor. 15), and almost nothing is said about Jesus' teaching, his life, and his birth or family connections. Brown calls for the recognition of this process so that modern readers do not suppose that the church's message is primarily about a child being born and the giving of gifts. "The process was literally an interpretative one of reading back later insights into the birth stories, and those later insights involved an adult Christ who had died and risen."[1]

John the Baptist Suffered Too (14:1–12; 17:9–13)

In chapter 2 the central place of John the Baptist in Matthew's Gospel has already been pointed out (pp. 16–17). The story of King Herod Antipas's dissolute indulgence and the fact that he had more concern about the opinion of his drunken courtiers (14:1–12) than the cause of justice allow Matthew to show how the gruesome torture and execution of John parallels what happened to Jesus in his infancy: that is, King Herod's (Antipas's father's) ruthless guarding of his kingship and the attempted murder of Jesus while he was still a toddler (2:13–18). Antipas's guilty conscience and his irrational thought that Jesus might be John raised from the dead illustrate the point that Matthew is making: what happens to John is awaiting Jesus. He is preparing the way, and it not only leads to suffering and death but to the resurrection to new life. The same concept is illustrated again in the story of the transfiguration in 17:1–13. There, Jesus compares John to one of the greatest of the Old Testament prophets, the one he imitated in his dress, speech, and message: " 'Elijah is indeed coming and will restore all things; but I tell you that Elijah has already come, and they did not recognize him, but they did to him whatever they pleased. So also the Son of Man is about to suffer at their hands.' Then the disciples understood that he was speaking to them about John the Baptist" (vv. 11–13).

Feeding of the Five Thousand (14:13–21)

Although the story of the feeding of the five thousand seems at first glance to be a simple miracle account about Jesus' incredible powers, it also pushes back into Old Testament prophecies and forward toward God's promises for the future. It would be difficult for a Jew to hear this story, for example, without thinking about the exodus, of how God brought the people out of Egyptian slavery and fed them with manna in the wilderness (see Exod. 16:1–12). For Matthew, Jesus is the new Moses who brings his people out of oppression and gives them the new commandments of God.

Christians, on the other hand, would think ahead about God's promise of the banquet for all of God's children at the end of time when the kingdom will finally be realized. Modern readers make a mistake if they try to focus on the miraculous aspects and merely try to explain how Jesus made so much food for so many people. Instead, attention should be paid to the fact that he was demonstrating how the promises that the children of God will be fed (both spiritually and physically) when the kingdom of heaven is inaugurated are being realized now in him. As Psalm 132:15 puts it, God has chosen Zion and says, "I will abundantly bless its provisions; / I will satisfy its poor with bread." Building on this image, Jesus foresaw a time when all of God's people would gather around one table: "'I tell you, many will come from east and west and will eat with Abraham and Isaac and Jacob in the kingdom of heaven'" (Matt. 8:11). For Jesus, this promise was being fulfilled in his ministry and will be realized all over the world when his disciples obey his commandment to feed the hungry, give drink to the thirsty, and clothe the naked (Matt. 25:31–46).

It is also possible to see how this feeding story provides another important symbol of the life of faith in the church. When Jesus ordered the disciples to feed the huge crowd—"'You give them something to eat'" (14:16)—Christian readers would automatically think of the Lord's Supper, which they celebrated every week. When Matthew says that Jesus broke the loaves, looked up to heaven, "and gave them to the disciples, and the disciples gave them to the crowds" (14:19), the liturgy of Holy Communion must have been in mind: "The Lord Jesus on the night when he was betrayed took a loaf of bread, and when he had given thanks, he broke it and said, 'This is my body that is for you. Do this in remembrance of me'" (1 Cor. 11:23–24).

Jesus Walks on the Sea (14:22–36)

As was noted above in chapter 3 (p. 25), the sea-crossing accounts (see Matt. 8:23–27) are important to all three of the Synoptic writers: Matthew, Mark, and Luke. This story finds parallel versions in Mark 6:45–52 and John 6:15–21, where Jesus also walks on the water. All three evangelists connect this incident to the account of the feeding of the five thousand, and in all three accounts the disciples are astounded that Jesus can do such a thing; they are extremely frightened. Matthew and Mark both report that they think Jesus is a "ghost" (Gk., *phantasma*). In Mark's Gospel the failure of the disciples to recognize Jesus on the sea is a sign of their unbelief and hardness of heart (Mark 6:45). In Matthew, on the other hand, even though it points to their "little faith," they are finally moved to worship him and confess him as the Son of God (Matt. 14:33).

Matthew has an additional section (14:28–33) in which Peter tries unsuccessfully to imitate Jesus' water walk, and it is worth some attention. In Matthew's account Peter believes that if Jesus commands him, he can also walk on the storming sea. When he receives the invitation "Come," he walks a short distance and then sinks. In Matthew this shows how doubt can prevent believers from following Jesus' example, especially in dangerous circumstances. But the readers know that this same Peter, even though he will deny Jesus on Good Friday (26:69–75), is also the one on whom Jesus will build the church, the Rock on which the faith will first stand (in Matt. 16:18, the word *petra* in Greek means "rock" or "stone"). The story of the storm at sea provides encouragement to believers in other times and places: even if they are sinking in doubt and discouragement, Peter's example demonstrates that those with little faith can still be called to do mighty acts.

The True Meaning of Being Clean (15:1–20; 16:1–12)

In these passages we see primary examples of what are often called "controversy narratives," that is, accounts that picture Jesus in conflict with the leading religious authorities of Israel, the Pharisees and Sadducees. The disagreements were not merely on an intellectual level but had important overtones for religious and political power and the search for the basic truth about the relationship between God and true believers. Since the religious authorities are the ones who agitated for Jesus' crucifixion, the nature of their debates with Jesus is important. See the discussion in chapter 4 (pp. 28–29) about the attacks they mount earlier in his ministry.

In chapter 15, Matthew bases his account on the debate in Mark 7:1–23 about ritual cleanliness. The argument is not only about the ritual of hand washing but about the proper interpretation of it. Jesus does not reject the commandments of the Scriptures as a whole but the twist that the Pharisees put on them: " 'Why do you break the commandment of God for the sake of your tradition?' " (15:3). The Jews of the first century CE regularly practiced cleansing ceremonies, as the discovery by archaeologists of baths called *mikvaoth* in public places and private homes all through Israel indicates (see Exod. 29:4; 30:17–21; 40:30–32; Lev. 8:6; 15; 16:4, 24; Pss. 26:6; 73:13; Isa. 1:15–18). According to Matthew and Mark, Jesus was not as concerned about the antiseptic character of Jewish rituals (being 99.9 percent germ free!), as he was about the necessity of becoming spiritually clean, purified from the inside out (Matt. 15:16–20). For Jesus' debate with the Pharisees about the need for a sign to prove that he has the right to reinterpret God's law, see the discussion above about a similar encounter in 12:38–45 (see p. 31).

Matthew's Version of Peter's Confession (16:13–20)

In chapter 16, Matthew returns to a portrayal of the central importance of Peter in the development of the church's mission (see the discussion of 14:22–36 above.) Once again he uses the basic account from Mark's Gospel, but with significant changes. In Mark 8:27–9:1, the evangelist shows that Peter, despite the fact that he acknowledges that Jesus is the Messiah (the Christ), does not really know what that means. When Jesus tells him that he must suffer, die, and be raised again, Peter rebukes him. Jesus in turn rebukes Peter and says, " 'Get behind me, Satan! For you are setting your mind not on divine things but on human things'" (Mark 8:33). Even though Peter follows Jesus throughout the rest of Mark's Gospel, he never fully understands who Jesus is or what he is about. He will not fully know what it means to call Jesus the Messiah or the Son of God until after the resurrection.

Although Matthew records a similar discussion between Jesus and Peter (Matt. 16:22–23), he modifies its impact significantly by introducing it with Jesus' praise of Peter's confession that he is the Christ and the Son of the living God. There, rather than rebuking Peter, Jesus blesses him and tells him that it is on him that he will build the church (16:15–19). For Matthew, Peter, despite his shortcomings, is the true leader of the first Christians. Peter sees who Jesus truly is long before the crucifixion and resurrection.

Predictions of Jesus' Passion, Resurrection, and Ascent to Power (16:21–28; 17:22–23; 20:17–19)

On three different occasions Jesus predicts what is to happen to him soon, how he will undergo "great suffering at the hands of the elders and the chief priests and scribes, and be killed, and on the third day be raised" (16:21). That the disciples are distressed at such an announcement (17:23) is completely understandable. How could God allow such things to happen to the Messiah, the one Peter calls "the Son of the living God"? Jesus answers this unspoken question with his understanding of the divine necessity of its happening (16:23). What will happen to him is not just bad luck, the result of the machinations of evil opponents, or the work of Satan. He shows them that he *must* (16:21) be betrayed into human hands. He *must* suffer, be crucified, and be raised, and he *must* come again in power after he returns to the Father. These events are all part of the promise of God that Jesus preached about from the very beginning of his ministry: to bring light out of darkness and life out of death, to inaugurate the kingdom of heaven, and to make possible the forgiveness of sins for those who turn and repent (4:16–17). Later writers, like the author of Hebrews, saw Jesus' suffering death as the fulfillment of God's promises in the Old Testament and evidence that he is truly the Messiah:

> He has appeared once for all at the end of the age to remove sin by the sacrifice of himself. And just as it is appointed for mortals to die once, and after that the judgment, so Christ, having been offered once to bear the sins of many, will appear a second time, not to deal with sin, but to save those who are eagerly awaiting him. (Heb. 9:26–28)

Although it is difficult to know when and where Jesus actually gave the passion predictions (some people think that they were added by the Gospel writers after the resurrection) it is not hard to imagine that he could have had instincts about what God would require of him or premonitions about what might happen. It would not have been difficult for him to guess what happens to people who publicly challenge powerful political and religious leaders. After all, we know from history that Abraham Lincoln had dreams that he would be assassinated and that Martin Luther King Jr. sensed in his great speech on the Mall in Washington, DC, that even if he led his people to the "promised land," he would not get there himself.

The Transfiguration (17:1–13)

The account of Jesus' encounter with God on the high mountain is traditionally called "the transfiguration" because Matthew and Luke report that he was transformed in a supernatural way right before the disciples' eyes (Matt. 17:1–13; Mark 9:2–13). The Greek word for "transfigured" is *metamorphoō*, the root from which we get our word *metamorphosis*, a complete change of form or structure. Matthew says that "his face shone like the sun, and his clothes became dazzling white" (17:2).

At that point the greatest prophets from the Old Testament (Moses and Elijah) appear and authenticate that Jesus' ministry is from God. As at the time of his baptism (3:17), God's voice speaks from the heavens (a cloud) and says, " 'This is my Son, the Beloved, with whom I am well pleased.' " For the first Christians this event again anchors Jesus in the past and propels him into the future. Jesus is like Moses, who received the commandments from God on the mountain out of thunder and smoke (Exod. 19:16–25). On the mount of transfiguration Jesus also appears as he will after the resurrection, looking like the angel who announces later that he is still alive, one whose "appearance was like lightning," whose clothing was "white as snow" (28:3). The last verse of chapter 16 prepares the reader for the setting of this divine stage where Jesus announces that he will come again at the end of the age in a new form: " 'For the Son of Man is to come with his angels in the glory of his Father, and then he will repay everyone for what has been done' " (16:27).

Demons, Epilepsy, and Little Faith (17:14–21)

This story, sometimes called "the epileptic boy cured" in modern Bible outlines, clearly shows the stark differences between ancient and contemporary concepts of illness and healing. In the first century CE people who came to Jesus for healing obviously did not know anything about the medical basis of epilepsy. As the father indicates, they could only imagine that some kind of an evil spirit caused the boy to foam at the mouth and thrash around. What Jesus may have known about the correct neurological diagnosis is uncertain. Perhaps he believed in demons himself and was convinced that the power of God could drive them out. If, on the other hand, he, as the Son of God, understood the true nature of the boy's illness, then it is possible that he acceded to the popular notion of demon possession so that the healing would not be totally beyond the understanding of the people he wanted to help. Without knowing more about his self-consciousness, modern readers must continue to ponder the question.

Regardless of which approach Jesus took, Matthew and Mark (Mark 9:14–29) make it clear that the little boy's was a difficult case to treat. After the high point of the transfiguration, Jesus has to come back down to earth and deal not only with a seemingly incurable situation but also with the ineptitude of the disciples, since the father reports that the disciples who remained in the valley were unable to do anything to help the little boy.

When the disciples ask why they could not heal the child, Jesus replies again that it has to do with "little faith" (17:20). Since he rebukes them for not even having confidence the size of a tiny mustard seed, all the faith that this kind of case would require, it must be that he considered their faith to be so small that it was nearly microscopic!

Administering the Church (18:1–35)

It is difficult to provide adequate background for this central passage in such a brief treatment as we are able to present here. In these verses Matthew reveals a great deal about his community of faith as he takes sayings of Jesus found in Mark, materials from another source scholars call "Q" (see the introduction, p. 5), and exhortations he may have composed himself to give advice to a church struggling with critical administrative and spiritual questions. Verse 17, " 'If the member refuses to listen to them, tell it to the church; and if the offender refuses to listen even to the church, let such a one be to you as a Gentile and a tax collector,' " sets the stage since the word "church" (Gk., *ecclesia*) is not one Jesus would have used prior to the time the Christian community was actually formed (after his death and resurrection). Whereas "church" appears numerous times in Acts, the letters of Paul, and in Hebrews, James, 3 John, and Revelation, it is only found in the Gospels twice, both times in Matthew (16:18; 18:17).

Although the sayings of Jesus here can be studied individually to try to determine what they meant in his time and situation, those who want to know what they signify to Matthew need to look at chapter 18 as a whole. For Matthew's church, important questions were brewing that had not yet been sorted out or solved, ones about the evangelism of new converts (18:1–7), keeping one's faith strong (18:8–9), restoring lapsed believers back into the church

(18:10–14), dealing with conflict within the community (18:15–20), and the nature and scope of forgiveness in the church (18:21–35).[2]

The last question in the chapter (18:21–35) was asked by Peter: " 'Lord . . . how often should I forgive?' " (v. 21). He is the one who is the spokesperson for the disciples and the leader who will create the foundation of the new community. Jesus says to him in 16:18, " 'You are Peter, and on this rock, I will build my church' " (*ekklēsia*). As a whole, the chapter and Jesus' answer in 18:21–35 demonstrate how far Jesus will go to make sure that those outside the faith (unbelievers or those who have stumbled) are restored as true children of God.

The final parable makes it clear. If a powerful human being like a rich king is willing to forgive a man for a debt amounting to millions of dollars, how much more will our heavenly father do for us? In order to make sure this happens, Matthew sternly reminds his readers of the law of reciprocity already found in the Lord's Prayer, where Jesus teaches his followers to ask God to forgive them with the same measure they forgive others (6:12): if you, like the borrower in the story, do not forgive other church members for the little amount they owe you, how can you expect God to forgive and accept you when you owe to God absolutely everything you have and are?

More Teaching Before Jerusalem: Transition (19:1–2)

These summary verses are similar to those found in 7:28, 11:1, and 13:53. Jesus now leaves his home area, Galilee on the west side of the Sea of Galilee, and heads into Judea. Judea, as Matthew seems to define it, refers to a small part of Palestine in and around Jerusalem, as distinguished from Galilee in the north and Samaria in the center of the country. The large crowds follow him, and he continues his healing ministry. Jesus' face is now set toward the capital city and certain conflict there.

The Test of Marriage (19:3–12)

This passage is troublesome for Christians today, and there is no easy way to interpret it comfortably. Here Jesus indicates that anyone who remarries after being divorced is guilty of breaking the commandment forbidding adultery (Exod. 20:13). This strict interpretation of Jewish law seems compatible with what he said in the Sermon on the Mount (5:27–32): that adultery involves more than sexual intercourse but also includes even looking with lust at another person. Considering the high rate of divorce in the twenty-first century and the constant scandals that involve politicians, athletes, entertainers, and even priests and pastors, how are we to understand this teaching today?

Some interpreters try to maneuver around the harshness of the text by arguing that it (and Mark 10:2–12) are not really the words of Jesus but come from a later source, added by later writers to help deal with problems of immorality in the early church (see 1 Cor. 5:1–5). But this is too easy a solution and a somewhat dishonest handling of the passage. If we take the words of Jesus at their face value, however, they remain extremely disturbing. Do they mean that all those who have divorced except for the possible reason of "unchastity" (5:31–32) are condemned to solitary lives and continuing unhappiness? Certainly Christians acknowledge the importance of commitment and the fact that marriage and sexual relationships are blessed by God (Gen. 1:26–28; 2:24–25). Nevertheless, knowing that Jesus urged reconciliation with God and other people and preached about a God of love, it is difficult to believe that he would deny millions of men and women the opportunity to start their lives anew. Those who have been divorced must take Jesus' teaching in these verses with utmost seriousness and admit their own responsibility for broken marriages, learn how to avoid making the same mistakes in new relationships, and move on, hoping and believing in the continuing grace of God in Jesus Christ.

The Problem of Many Possessions (19:16–30)

The difficulty with this incident in Jesus' life is similar to the teaching about adultery in 19:3–12; modern readers wonder whether it should be taken literally or not. Did Jesus really mean that it will be difficult or impossible for the rich to enter the kingdom of heaven, or was he using hyperbole again to make a point?

The evidence indicates that Jesus (and Matthew) intends the warning about the danger of riches to be taken seriously. The conversation is between Jesus and a young man (v. 22) about the meaning of the Ten Commandments. When the man is asked whether he has kept them all, he can honestly answer in the affirmative. But when Jesus adds another requirement, namely, that he is to give away his possessions, the seeker is finished, because he cannot part with all the money and things he values so much.

Attempts to soften this teaching by indicating that the needle's eye is a gate in the ancient wall of Jerusalem are bogus. The gate, "the needle's eye," did not exist in the first century CE, and the needle in Jesus' story is a simple sewing needle. Obviously no animal (or person) can squeeze through this tiny opening, and Jesus concludes that it will be "hard" (Gk., *duskolos*), if not impossible, for people with a lot of money to get into the kingdom.

This was bad news for many of the elite political and religious leaders of Jesus' day because most of them were at the top of the economic pyramid. They lived in the plush homes found by archaeologists on the hills above the Temple Mount (destroyed by the Romans in 70 CE). They and business people who regularly exploited the poor were warned by Jesus that they already had their reward. In the alternative kingdom that he was establishing, "bottom man will be on top," as the American slaves used to say, and the rich will lose more than their money, houses, and investments; they will also lose their souls, for what is at stake finally is "salvation," that is, eternal forgiveness and redemption by God.

If this judgment seems harsh for Jesus' contemporaries, it may be even more difficult for those of us living in the twenty-first century. To those who love their homes and cars and expensive vacations more than God, Jesus appears to have a simple and frightening message: you will never be in the kingdom of heaven. (For the concerns of the early church about the dangers of wealth, see Matt. 5:3; 7:19–34; Luke 6:20–25; Acts 4:32–37; 11:27–29; Rom. 15:22–29; 1 Tim. 6:10; Jas. 5:1–6.)

Parable of the Landowner (20:1–16)

The narrative of the Rich Young Ruler ends with the enigmatic statement in 19:30, "'Many who are first will be last, and the last will be first,'" and serves as a link to the following story about agricultural workers being paid the same wage regardless of what time they arrived in the fields.

Generally, biblical scholars have interpreted this parable symbolically as an illustration of the fact that God's bounty depends entirely on God's grace and mercy rather than human standards of fairness (see Exod. 33:19; Rom. 9:15–18 for examples). Often it is understood as a validation of the Protestant emphasis on grace rather than works (Gal. 2:15–21; Rom. 3:21–31) or a vindication of the early Christian argument that Gentiles should be welcomed into the church as true children of God. The parable seemed to indicate Jesus' belief that it does not matter when you come to God, or if you are part of the chosen people, newcomers or outsiders. All that counts is that God accepts you whenever God pleases; grace is at work 24/7.

Recently, another approach has been suggested that uses economic, anthropological, and sociological models of study and seems more consistent with Matthew's concern about the dangers of wealth. William Herzog II, for example, argues that Jesus used parables like this one as "subversive speech," that is, as subtle ways to condemn the rich landowners connected with King Herod and the elite religious leaders in Jerusalem. This parable, rather than showing what God is like, Herzog contends, demonstrates how patronizing landowners were, how they were arbitrary and parsimonious in the payment of wages, and how difficult it was to be a day laborer and hope that one could feed a family based only on the whims of the owner.[3] By examining Jesus' parables from economic and cultural perspectives, an entirely new understanding of his teaching becomes possible. New forms of ministry are suggested as the church of the twenty-first century reaches out to those who have lost their jobs, their homes, and their medical benefits because of the exploitation and fraud of dishonest corporate and government officials.

Power Play (20:17–28)

Following the last of Jesus' three predictions about his impending suffering, death, and resurrection in 20:17–19 (see the discussion above in this chapter, pp. 40–41), Matthew turns to an incredible narrative in 20:20–28 about the blatant ambitions of two disciples as Jesus closes in on his destiny at Golgotha. In Mark's version it is said that the brothers James and John approached Jesus about places of honor in the coming kingdom (Mark 10:35–40). In Matthew it is their mother who asks a favor of him: " 'Declare that these two sons of mine will sit, one at your right hand and one at your left, in your kingdom' " (20:21). Matthew's change may cast primary blame on their mother (*cherchez la femme!*) because, unlike Mark, he does not want this incident to focus on the disciples' blindness and ignorance. When Jesus asks if they are able to drink his cup of suffering they naively reply, " 'We are able' " (20:21), not fully understanding what Jesus has to face (or the fact that places of honor in the kingdom are for God to decide, not him).

In both Matthew and Mark the passage concludes with a discourse about the different ways power is used in this world and the kingdom to come. As the parable of the Landowner demonstrates, people with money and influence like to tyrannize those who are under them (Matt. 20:25), but it is not to be that way with Jesus' followers (or the members of Matthew's church): "Whoever wishes to be first among you must be your slave; just as the Son of Man came not to be served but to serve, and give his life as a ransom for many" (20:27–28).

Two Blind Men Follow Jesus (20:29–34)

In the final story before Jesus' entry into Jerusalem, Matthew presents the healing narrative about two blind men from Jericho who follow Jesus, presumably into the capital. Jericho is an ancient city a few miles northeast of Jerusalem, and the main north-south road passed through there. In Mark's Gospel this story provides a critical transition in the passion narrative as a blind man named Bartimaeus is healed and follows Jesus "on the way," that is, the way of the Lord, the way of the cross (Mark 10:46–52). Matthew removes the name of the patient (perhaps he was not known in Matthew's community) and doubles the number of people healed.

He does the same thing in 8:28–9:1 where the Markan demoniac named "Legion" now becomes two crazed men healed of their affliction. Matthew tells a similar story about two blind men in 9:27–31, which is only found in his Gospel. By doubling the number of recipients who receive Jesus' attentions Matthew may wish to double the impact of Jesus' power on his readers. In the final verse, Matthew also reinterprets the main point of the story: instead of being about blindness and discipleship as it is in Mark, it now illustrates the "mercy" of God and Jesus' love of the sick and poor: "Moved with compassion, Jesus touched their eyes. Immediately they regained their sight and followed him" (see Matt. 9:35–36; 15:32; 14:14).

Notes

1. Raymond E. Brown, *An Adult Christ at Christmas: Essays on Three Biblical Stories* (Collegeville, MN: Liturgical Pres, 1977), 8.
2. I have made an attempt to show how Matthew 18 provides guidance for conflict among modern church members. See Earl S. Johnson Jr., *Selected To Serve: A Guide For Church Officers* (Louisville, KY: Geneva Press, 2000), 77–93.
3. William R. Herzog III, *Prophet and Teacher: An Introduction to the Historical Jesus* (Louisville, KY: Westminster John Knox Press, 2005), 151.

Chapter Six

The Messiah in God's City

A Study of Matthew 21:1–27:66

A New Empire Visible (21:1–16)

Palm Sunday is traditionally a day of celebration and excitement in the Christian church when Jesus' triumphant entry into the capital city is commemorated. The cheers of support in verse 9 " 'Hosanna to the Son of David! / Blessed is the one who comes in the name of the Lord! / Hosanna in the highest heaven!' " echo the words of thanksgiving to God in Psalm 118:26 that proclaim that God has become salvation to the people. As a result, the psalmist anticipates a great celebration in the sanctuary:

> The LORD is God,
>   and he has given us light.
> Bind the festal procession with branches,
>   up to the horns of the altar. (Ps. 118:27)

The exaltation "hosanna" is from two Hebrew words that mean "Save, we pray" and anticipates the coming of the Messiah. The impression the story gives is that some of the people in Jerusalem knew who Jesus was and celebrated his arrival during Passover week.

Generally this passage has been understood to underscore Jesus' humility and his unwillingness to call attention to himself. This impression is strengthened by Matthew's quotation in verse 5 of two Old Testament texts from Isaiah 62:11 and Zechariah 9:9: "humble, and mounted on a donkey, and on a foal, the colt of a donkey." Yet this can be misleading.

Certainly Jesus did not come into the city as a Roman governor might, with fanfare and a compliment of armed soldiers. He did not ride down the main street like a general celebrating a military victory. But it is also clear that he did not sneak into Jerusalem unnoticed without making a claim for himself. In fact, he deliberately took the road still clearly visible from the city walls today, from Bethphage at the top of the Mount of Olives (north of the Intercontinental Hotel in modern Jerusalem) to opposite the Golden Gate (which was closed by Muslim conquerors long ago). What is more, it is also clear that he entered not as a humble supplicant but as a king, as one who would challenge Roman authority by taking the same road used by Solomon prior to his investiture. As 1 Kings 1:32–40 relates it, King David had his son ride his mule down to Gihon, and all the people followed him, rejoicing with great joy. (Gihon is the major spring in Jerusalem located in the Kidron Valley at the bottom of the Mount of Olives.)

The spreading of the clothes on the way is misunderstood, moreover, if it is merely seen as the efforts of the poor to honor a would-be prophet. Before Jehu became king (2 Kgs. 9:11–13), his followers "all took their cloaks and spread them for him . . . and they blew the trumpet, and proclaimed, 'Jehu is king.'"

Verse 9 fortifies this impression as the people chant the words from Psalm 118:15–27, where it is said that God will be victorious when the gates of righteousness are opened. The stone that the builder rejected will become the cornerstone, and the Lord's doings will become marvelous in the people's eyes. Clearly, as the next few chapters indicate, Jesus did not enter Jerusalem as a king determined to overthrow the Roman government by military force. But he did arrive as a prophet-king who would demand justice and righteousness for the people. As Psalm 118:15, 19 puts it,

> There are glad songs of victory in
>   the tents of the righteous:
> "The right hand of the LORD does valiantly;
>   the right hand of the Lord is exalted; . . ."
> . . . .
> Open to me the gates of righteousness,
>   that I may enter through them
>   and give thanks to the LORD.

It is no wonder, therefore, that Matthew reports Jerusalem was in turmoil. It is as if the people asked, "Who is this person? Is he a prophet who comes in like a king and promises an alternative empire?"

Cleansing the Temple (21:12–46)

It is not difficult to see how Jesus' challenge to power is reinforced by the account of the cleansing of the Temple, the encounter of a fig tree withered by him, the continuing challenges of the religious authorities, and the parables that follow in 21:28–46.

The impressive Temple built by King Herod the Great, one of the largest that existed anywhere in the world during the first century CE, took years to construct and at one time probably employed more that 18,000 people. This rebuilding (a structure was already on the site in Jerusalem) was a tremendous undertaking. As Peter Richardson describes it, "The rebuilding's organization and careful preparations, the quality and the enormous quantities of materials used, the vast scale and drama of the Temple, its innovations, its integration into the existing cityscape, the demand to continue regular worship—all are truly staggering."[1] Some of its massive blocks weighing several tons each can still be seen today, uncovered by archaeologists on the first-century road next to the Western Wall.

All four Gospel writers indicate, of course, that Jesus was not impressed. Especially disturbing to him was the administration of the Temple, in particular the way that offerings could only be made by using special money that had to be purchased at inflated exchange rates. Jesus' anger at turning God's house of prayer into a den of crooks (see Isa. 56:7) may remind modern readers of the disgust they feel with high rates of interest charged on credit cards, the hidden costs of calls on cell phones, the high price of medical services, and the exorbitant salaries given to corporate executives. Sometimes people just do not want to take it anymore. The fact that Jesus' anger about such a lack of respect for God's house led him to express himself violently in protest (turning over the tables and causing a commotion) is taken up symbolically in the next passage by Matthew (21:18–22) and Mark (11:12–14) with the story of the fig tree killed by Jesus. Whether or not the tree could really be expected to bear fruit in the early spring seems beside the point. The fig tree, as a symbol of Israel (Jer. 24:1–10; 29:17; Hos. 2:12; Joel 1:7; Mic. 7:1–3, and so on), and because of Israel's current lack of faith (fruit), is dramatically destroyed to show what will happen to those who do not turn back to God and offer true worship.

Jesus' Authority Challenged Again and Again and Again (21:23–27; 22:23–45; 23:1–38)

When Jesus enters the Temple precinct a second time after the cursing of the fig tree, representatives of the leaders of the major religious parties surround him and demand to know by whose authority he threatens their administration. For them, it is a matter of power and influence, and they want him stopped, especially during the time of Passover when so many people are crowded into the city. Jesus' reply leaves them dissatisfied and stumped since he only answers them with a riddle about the popularity of John the Baptist and whether or not he came from God. They cannot answer without losing face because John was so popular among the people, so he does not answer their question either.

In the following chapters, Matthew continues to show the mounting resistance and hostility to Jesus that leads to their decision to recruit Judas Iscariot and to have Jesus arrested: in the debate about the meaning of the resurrection (21:23–32), in the controversy about the great commandment (22: 33–40), in the discussion about the true meaning of the title "the Son of David" (22:41–46), and in Jesus' continuing challenges aimed at the Pharisees in the whole of chapter 23.

The Kingdom Will Be Taken Away from You (21:28–46)

Although there is insufficient space in this brief presentation to examine each of the passages in detail in which Jesus is threatened by the religious authorities, the two parables at the end of chapter 21 point to the common thread in his response to their attacks. Verse 43 provides a key to Jesus' thinking in Matthew when he warns, " 'Therefore I tell you, the kingdom of God will be taken away from you and given to a people that produces the fruits of the kingdom.' " The story of the two sons, one who only talked about doing the father's wishes and the other who really carried them out, points to the failure of many people to recognize who Jesus was. They talked good religion and professed to serve God, but when the Father sent the Son with the message that would save them, they did not believe him.

Similarly in 21:33–46, in the story of the Wicked Tenants, and in the following parable of the Wedding Banquet (22:1–14), a very strong impression is given that by rejecting God's true prophet, the prophet of justice and righteousness, the one who truly is the Son, the people will be rejected, broken, and excluded from the final great banquet.

All about Money (22: 15–46)

Jesus' debate about money and the image of Caesar on a Roman denarius points to his continuing rejection of economic oppression of the people and the expansion of power to wealthy religious and political authorities. When the Pharisees and Herodians try to trick him into making a statement that will get him into trouble by asking whether or not Jews should pay Roman taxes, he simply replies, "'Give therefore to the emperor the things that are the emperor's and to God the things that are God's'" (22:21).

Although this passage is often discussed in the United States in the context of the constitutional separation of church and state, there are reasons to reconsider this traditional interpretation of the passage. Jesus seems to duck the hard question about taxation here, and the fact that he has to ask for a coin ("'Show me the coin used for the tax'" [22:19]) indicates that he did not even carry Roman money with him. Partly this was because he and his disciples supported themselves with gifts from supporters and the money gathered from begging, and partly because many Jews did not want to use a coin with a human image on it to pay taxes or for anything else because it violated the second commandment against the worship of idols (Exod. 20:4–6). In addition, since the reign of Augustus Caesar (27 BCE–14 CE), Roman coins often carried an inscription that pointed to the divine origin of the Roman emperor (emperors were routinely elevated to the status of a god by the Roman Senate after their deaths). Such a thought was reprehensible to faithful Jews. Moreover, by the time Matthew's Gospel was written (after 70 CE), Emperor Nero Claudius Caesar Augustus Germanicus (54–68 CE) had proclaimed on his coins that he was already a "son of god" and a living god himself.

For Matthew's readers it would have been repulsive to use such coins, and it is likely that they did not take Jesus' remarks as equivocal at all. If Jesus truly wanted to live in an empire invested in the righteousness and justice of God rather than one ruled by the power of wealthy men who thought they were divine, his remarks about giving to God what is God's could be understood in a radical way. Since God is the ruler of all nations and the kingdom of God is at hand, it was not necessary to give any homage or worship to the Roman emperor at all. From this perspective, regardless of how things seemed, the faithful Jews in Jesus' day, and the Christians in Matthew's, did not have to give the emperor anything since everything belonged to God in the first place. That the Pharisees and Herodians were amazed at such teaching is not surprising; they were totally invested in the secular power of Rome, and without such a connection they would not survive.

Apocalypse Now? (24:1–25:13)

The accounts of the coming of the end time found in these verses and in Luke 21:1–37 are largely based on Mark's apocalypse in Mark 13:1–37. The word *apocalypse* refers to a kind of Jewish and Christian writing that claims to have messages from God about the future: in these cases, about the impending destruction of Jerusalem, wars and rumors of wars, earthquakes, famines, persecution, the tribulation, and the second coming of the Messiah (the appearance of the Son of Man on the clouds). The same kind of description is applied to the last book of the New Testament where the word "Revelation" is used for its title (*apokalupis* in Greek means "revelation," "disclosure," "opening of secrets and mysteries"). Similar kinds of writings are found in the Old Testament in Daniel, Ezekiel, Zechariah, and other places.

This portion of Matthew is particularly difficult to understand because Bible scholars and historians have debated for a long time about its historical accuracy. Although it is entirely possible that Jesus as the Son of God could have easily foreseen the disasters that awaited the people of Israel if they did not repent and return to God, many scholars wonder if the bulk of this material was not written after 70 CE, some forty years after Jesus' death, following the destruction of Jerusalem and the Temple by the Roman armies of General Vespasian and his son Titus.

The "stones" mentioned in Matthew 24:2, for example, seem to describe the complete destruction of the Temple and the way the Romans pried loose the huge building blocks constructed by Herod's workman and cast them down pell-mell into the streets below. They can still be seen there where archaeologists discovered them near the Western Wall.

The "desolating sacrilege" mentioned in 24:15, furthermore, could refer back to Daniel 9:27 and later Jewish concerns about the "abomination of desolation" when King Antiochus Epiphanes IV destroyed the Holy of Holies around 167 BCE. But it also could be a description of the systematic destruction of the entire Temple Mount by the Romans in order to demoralize and embarrass the Jews, for whom the Temple served as their spiritual and political center. The symbol of the menorah from the Temple on Titus's triumphal arch in Rome (still visible today) shows how humiliating the Roman conquest was.

This chapter and other passages like it in the New Testament (see Rom. 13:11–14; Jas. 5:7–11; Heb. 10:25; 1 Pet. 4:7) that predict the second coming of the Son of God or the *parousia* (coming again) of the Messiah also need to be studied very carefully by believers today because of the continuing prophecies of the end of the world and those that surfaced recently at the beginning of the twenty-first century in the year 2000 and again in reference to 2012. Many Christians living in the first century CE obviously took literally the words of Jesus in Matthew 16:27 and 26:29 (and similar passages in Mark and Luke) and expected that he would return to judge the world before their generation passed away. Paul also seems to have understood the situation in this way, but as 1 Thessalonians 5:1–11 demonstrates, he had to recalculate his own expectations because Jesus' return did not happen when it was anticipated.

Words attributed to Jesus in Matthew 24:36–44 indicate that he also did not know when the end would come, since it would arrive unannounced like a thief in the night (see the parables of the Unprepared Slaves in 24:50 and of the Ten Bridesmaids in 25:1–13, especially v. 13).

As Jesus says in 24:36, " 'But about that day and hour no one knows, neither the angels of heaven, nor the Son, but only the Father.' " Apparently the first Christians misunderstood Jesus' teaching and expected him to return momentarily when that was not what he meant. Christians today should learn from their experience and be careful not to be swayed by modern false prophets who claim to know more than the first followers of Jesus did.

Jesus' Central Teaching (25:14–30; 25:31–46)

The parable of the Talents and Jesus' teaching about helping those in need follow immediately after the discussion of the apocalypse and indicate that Matthew and his readers did not expect the world to end any time soon. Instead, Jesus teaches them to invest in the future and to be ready at all times to help those who are oppressed or without the basic resources of life. Both of these passages provide important insights into what Matthew was thinking since they are only found in his Gospel and they occur right before the central account of Jesus' arrest and crucifixion.

Traditionally, the parable of the Talents is understood in terms of using the gifts that God gives to believers and the punishment that can come if the gifts are squandered. The failure to invest one's talents symbolizes the fact that who we are and what we have are gifts from God that are expected to be used in the right way and for the right purpose in the kingdom.

In Jesus' story a *talent* does not refer to a special natural ability or aptitude, as the English word suggests, but is a Jewish unit of money measured by weight. In New Testament times a talent was over 58 kg, or more than 125 pounds of silver or gold. In modern terms we can see that if gold sells for more than $1,000 an ounce, five talents would be more than $10 million, an enormous sum for anyone to have, much less a slave.

Once again we can see that Jesus likes to tell stories that are exaggerated for effect, given to hyperbole so much that they are not easily forgotten. In the parable, therefore, he is not trying to teach that believers will be rich if they invest in the stock market or that they can actually get that kind of money if they are faithful, but that God expects us to use our valuable gifts, whatever they are, for the work of the kingdom. How that is to happen is made clear in the following story about the separation of the sheep and the goats (vv. 31–33.)

In reference to the parable of the Talents it can be noted that it not only provides insights into what Matthew expected of the members of the church but also provides valuable information about the economic situation in Palestine in the first century CE. It demonstrates that there were people who had enormous amounts of money and who owned slaves, and they could do whatever they wanted with their money and with those who worked for them. Readers who are interested in this aspect of the Gospel can examine important studies that explore ancient economics, social stratification, the value of money, taxation, and the roles of slaves and peasants.[2]

Many Bible scholars and Christian believers think that Matthew 25:31–46 is one of the most important passages in Matthew's account of Jesus' life and teaching (or possibly in the whole Bible), and with good reason. In this central passage Matthew provides Jesus' instruction about the main criterion that defines who his followers really are and what they must do.

The story is set in the context of a scene that Matthew's readers might have observed at any time. Even today in modern Israel or Palestine, it is not uncommon to go to an outdoor village market where sheep and goats are waiting to be bought and sold, all separated into their own places. Using an image that his hearers could readily understand, therefore, Jesus provides them with another story about a king.

In this parable, one that is often quoted in sermons and even in political speeches today, the now-familiar account of how people are designated for paradise or eternal suffering is laid out graphically. The interesting thing about the way Jesus tells the story is that he assumes that doing the right thing, doing the good thing, doing the humane thing—that is, feeding the hungry, giving water to the thirsty, and clothing the naked—is the normal behavior, the expected behavior. Helping others, in Jesus' name, therefore, is not unusual or extraordinary activity; it is what God expects. What is unusual is disinterest, the avoidance of those who are oppressed or hurt by natural disasters or war. What are unusual are greed, a lack of generosity, and the unwillingness to share the gifts God has given. The end result for such people, as the parable of the Talents warns when it describes what happens to the one who hides his talents in a hole, is separation from God and eternal damnation (25:29, 46).

Ironically, those who do the right thing perform their acts of charity so naturally that they are not even aware of them, and they must ask, " 'When was it that we saw you hungry and gave you food?' " (25:37). And the king replies, " 'Truly I tell you, just as you did it to the least of these who are members of my family, you did it to me' " (25:40).

This teaching of Jesus is one that millions of believers throughout the centuries have taken literally. For them it has become a way of life and has been understood exactly as something they must do. Recently, just before he died, Senator Edward Kennedy expressed how important this passage was to him throughout his life, and his comments show how important this parable has been for the forming of private action as well as public policy.

> My own center of belief, as I matured . . . moved toward the great Gospel of
> Matthew, chapter 25 especially, in which he calls us to care for the least of these

among us. . . . To me, this perspective on my faith has almost literally been a life-saver. It has given me strength and purpose during the greatest challenges I have faced, and the roughest roads I've traveled.[3]

The Significance of the Last Supper (26:17–29)

Matthew, along with Mark and Luke, describe Jesus' observance of the Jewish annual celebration of the Passover ("the first day of Unleavened Bread," v. 17; see Exod. 12) as the prelude to his arrest, trial, and crucifixion. The last meal he has with the disciples is set in the context of the betrayal by Judas Iscariot, who made a deal with the chief priests for thirty pieces of silver to turn Jesus over to them. Matthew gives no motive for this cowardly act, although John says that he was the one who was most upset about Mary's purchase of expensive ointment (John 12:1–11). Generally, the Gospel writers are not interested in offering psychological explanations for Judas's behavior. Luke and John report that Satan made him do it (Luke 22:3; John 13:2; 6:70), and John adds that he was a thief (12:6) and did not care about the poor at all. After he betrays Jesus with a kiss (Matt. 26:48–50), he has second thoughts about his actions and commits suicide (27:3–10).

In Matthew's subsequent description of the celebration of the Passover, it is suggested that Jesus is the sacrificial lamb whose death takes away the sins of the world. Jesus' words, " 'Take, eat, this is my body' " (v. 26) and " 'This is my blood of the covenant,' " (v. 28) are very close to the liturgy of the Lord's Supper, which is celebrated regularly by Christians all over the world (also see 1 Cor. 11:23–32).

Garden of Gethsemane (26:36–56)

After Judas leaves and the Passover is completed, Jesus and the rest of the disciples go to the Garden of Gethsemane at the foot of the Mount of Olives, a kind of public park, where they are presumably going to rest for the night. But Jesus knows better. As he agonizes in prayer, recognizing that the time of his suffering is almost upon him, Peter, James, and John are unable to support him in his moment of agony and keep falling asleep. It is here that Peter utters the first of his three denials, even though he had previously declared his unequivocal loyalty to Jesus: " 'Even though I must die with you, I will not deny you.' And so said all the disciples" (v. 35).

Visitors to Jerusalem today can find public access to two ancient gardens and olive groves in the Kidron Valley just outside of the eastern wall of Jerusalem and gain a clear impression of what it must have been like for Jesus to have been in distress in Gethsemane as the busy city moved all around him during the night.

Hearings and Betrayals (26:47–56)

When Judas returns, he does not come alone. This time he brings a large armed crowd (undercover soldiers?) who are prepared to arrest Jesus as soon as he is identified. Judas does it with a cordial greeting, which is a sign of affection, the ultimate insult.

When they grab him, Jesus makes it clear that no violence is to be tolerated on the part of his disciples. One of the disciples hacks off the ear of the chief priest's slave with a sword (John 18:10 states that it was Peter), but Jesus orders him to stop. Even though he could have twelve legions of angels (about 72,000 of them) at his disposal, he only authorizes a nonviolent response. For him, this is all part of what God has already decreed and Old Testament prophets have forseen.

The first hearing of the charges against Jesus is held at the house of Caiaphas the high priest located in the rich part of the city above the Temple Mount. Joseph Caiaphas, appointed by the Romans, held office from 18–37 CE until he was removed by Pontius Pilate's successor, Vitellius Gratus. (A few years ago archaeologists discovered a tomb in Jerusalem containing an ossuary with Caiaphas's name on it in which his bones had been buried.) It was politically correct to send Jesus to him, because other than the king, he was the highest-ranking spiritual and political official in Palestine. The chief priests and scribes bring charges against Jesus and want Caiaphas to condemn Jesus to death, but the hearing is inconclusive since the Jews did not have the power to make capital convictions.

Jesus' opponents accuse him of saying that he would destroy the Temple and rebuild it in three days, claiming that he was the Messiah. When the high priest asks him point blank if he is the Messiah, Jesus laconically replies, " 'You have said so' " (v. 64). The high priest ceremoniously tears his clothes and accuses Jesus of blasphemy. Thus, the torturing begins as the guards slap and mock him.

In verses 69–75 Matthew describes the three times that Peter denies Jesus when bystanders question him. Even though his northern accent makes it clear that he comes from Jesus' home area of Galilee, he is so determined not to be connected to Jesus that he even begins to curse and swear for effect, and he vows before God that he does not know him. All this happens before the time when roosters usually begin to crow in the morning, and Peter is so ashamed of himself that he weeps uncontrollably.

Those wishing to see the site traditionally associated with this event can visit the Church of St. Peter in Gallicantu (cock crowing) in Jerusalem.

Crucifixion and Death (27:11–66)

In many ways this chapter and the one that follows describing Jesus' resurrection and ascension are the most important in Matthew's Gospel. As was mentioned in chapter 5, the early Christians usually told the story of Jesus' life and ministry backward, starting with the critical events at the end of his life and working back from there. The crucifixion and resurrection demonstrated most clearly to believers that Jesus was the Son of God and the Messiah; thus they received primary emphasis. As Paul put it in Galatians 2:19–20, "I have been crucified with Christ; and it is no longer I who live, but it is Christ who lives in me."

Before the description of Jesus' execution all four of the evangelists report Jesus' hearing before Pontius Pilate. Although the NRSV refers to him as the "governor," he was actually the prefect of the province (possibly appointed directly by the emperor) for ten years, from 26–36 CE. His term was the second longest in that office, and Flavius Josephus, a Jewish writer who turned from being a rebel general to a Roman supporter, writes extensively about Pilate's skill as a politician, his cruelty, and his disdain for the Jews. In 1961 a portion of a memorial stone dedicated by Pilate was discovered in the ruins of a Roman theater at Caesarea Maritima, and it bears the inscription *praefectus iudaeae* (Prefect of Judea). It can be seen in the Israel Museum in Jerusalem.

Although Matthew, Mark, and Luke all substantially report the same transcript of the trial, Matthew alone presents the account of Pilate's reception of a warning message from his wife (Matt. 27:19) and his seeming desire to absolve himself of any guilt for Jesus' execution when he washes his hands of the whole matter (27:24–26). Many historians and biblical scholars find this account to be at variance with the general impression provided by Josephus about the prefect and think it may be an attempt to remove the blame for Jesus' death from the Romans and place it more squarely on his Jewish opponents. Matthew and Mark report, furthermore, that Pilate offered the Jewish crowd in Jerusalem a choice between Jesus of Nazareth and Jesus Barabbas, the revolutionary, citing a custom that the governor could release one prisoner from a capital offense during Passover. Little, if any, historical evidence exists, however, to verify the existence of this custom.

Matthew also includes a disturbing encounter between the Jewish crowd and Pilate in 27:24–26 where they demand Jesus of Nazareth's execution so vociferously that they take full responsibility for his death. When Pilate claims that he is innocent of Jesus' blood, they reply, " 'His blood be on us and on our children!' " Although it is not clear exactly why Matthew reports this incident—whether he was trying to say that it was the rabble-rousers in Jerusalem who were the main instigators of Jesus' death sentence or whether he is blaming the incident on all the Jewish people—modern readers need to be careful how they read, teach, and preach this passage. This text, among others in the New Testament, has often been used to fan anti-Semitic paranoia and hatred, and such sentiments cannot be tolerated, whether coming from Christians or from anyone else living in a world that understands the need for mutual understanding and religious diversity. Regardless of what really happened, readers of Matthew must be aware of the history of interpretation of certain biblical texts and how they must be used sensitively now so that they do not create animosity between Jews and Christians in the future.

In regard to Jesus' crucifixion it is necessary to understand that his execution was not an unusual one in the ancient world. Various forms and shapes of crosses were used for centuries to punish prisoners and subjugate conquered nations. The Romans regularly used crucifixion as a deterrent to discourage people from crime or treason against the imperial government. Generally, the Romans only employed this mode of punishment against foreigners and non-citizens, for it was too demeaning for a citizen to bear. Tradition suggests, for example, that Peter, a Jew from Galilee, was crucified but that Paul, a Roman citizen by birth, died in some other way.

The Gospel writers appear to be quite accurate in their description of how the execution took place. Prisoners were tied or nailed to the cross after being beaten (for certain types of soldiers this part might have been considered entertaining). Prior to that, the condemned ones were often forced to carry their own cross beam (not the entire cross. which would have been too heavy). The execution squads were usually commanded by a centurion, an officer equivalent in modern armies to a master sergeant or a captain, one with extensive service and respect in the military. The crosses were set up in a public place (outside the city in Jesus' case) so that the victims' humiliation would be complete. Often their bodies were not taken down for days or weeks to reinforce the message about what would happen to anyone who defied Rome.

In Jesus' case, the Synoptic Gospels report that he died on Friday afternoon and his body was removed immediately thereafter, probably because it would be a violation of the Jewish Sabbath (which would begin in early evening) to do the work of handling or burying a corpse.

Some of the details of Jesus' death were seen by early Christians to be a fulfillment of Old Testament prophecies. Psalm 22 and the portrayal of the intense suffering of the messianic figure, the mocking of his opponents, the cry of pain, and even the dividing of the clothes of the victim among the guards by casting dice, came particularly to mind.

The fact that Jesus did not die a unique death but one that thousands of innocent victims suffered did not prevent early Christians from seeing his singularity. For them, it showed how Jesus had solidarity with the poor and oppressed people that he helped throughout his lifetime, how he was not afraid of the powers and principalities that rule this world, and how he obeyed God's will even if it meant he had to sacrifice his life for others. For Christians, it was amazing that God's own Son would undergo such humiliation and suffering to ransom many, and the cross, rather than being a sign of degradation, became a symbol of hope. As Paul wrote in Philippians 2:7–8,

> And being found in human form,
>> he humbled himself
>> and became obedient to the point of death—
>> even death on a cross.

Notes

1. Peter Richardson, *Herod, King of the Jews and Friend of the Romans* (Columbia, SC: University of South Carolina Press, 1996), 185. See Richardson's descriptions of the many other temples Herod build in honor of pagan gods and for the Roman emperors. Also see Duane W. Roller, *The Building Program of Herod the Great* (Berkeley, CA: University of California Press, 1998).
2. See, for example, Donald E. Oakman, *Jesus and the Peasants*, Matrix: The Bible in the Mediterranean Context 4 (Eugene, OR: Cascade Books, 2008).
3. Edward M. Kennedy, *True Compass: A Memoir* (New York: Hachette Book Group, 2009), 29–30.

Chapter Seven

Resurrection and the Birth of the Church

A Study of Matthew 28:1–20

Matthew's account of Jesus' resurrection, while based primarily on Mark 16:1–8, differs significantly from Mark's final chapter. Clearly Mark's conclusion of the resurrection story is based on a considerably different tradition, for his account ends enigmatically with the women running fearfully from the empty tomb; in Matthew 28:8–10, however, the risen Jesus meets the women and directs them to find the other disciples. Matthew also provides additional details as he includes the account of the bribing of the soldiers (28:11–15) and Jesus' proclamation of the "Great Commission" (28:16–20). The last two sections are found in none of the other Gospels. There is no evidence that Matthew is aware of the account of Jesus' ascension in Luke 24:50–53 and Acts 1:6–11.

Centrality of the Resurrection

Although Matthew's account of Jesus' resurrection is only ten verses, it plays a central role in overall structure of the Gospel. Jesus' suffering, death, and resurrection have been anticipated from the very beginning. It is with the messages of angels, for example (1:20–21; 2:13, 19), and an unusual natural phenomenon (the star in the east, 2:2) that the Gospel begins. Here it ends similarly, with "a great earthquake" and with "an angel of the Lord, descending from heaven" (28:2) to announce the fact that God has raised Jesus from the dead. The angel once again tells the hearers not to be afraid (see 1:20) and announces, " 'I know that you are looking for Jesus who was crucified. He is not here; for he has been raised, as he said. Come, see the place where he lay' " (28:6). Instructions are then given to go to Galilee, as Jesus told them earlier (26:32).

When Christians celebrate Easter they often combine the various resurrection accounts of the four evangelists without realizing how unique each account is. Mark's Gospel, for example, does not record any appearance of the resurrected Jesus, and therefore he says nothing to the astonished disciples. Scholars have concluded that the most reliable text ends in Mark 16:8 with the enigmatic words (if they were translated literally from the Greek) "they were afraid, but . . ." Although the New Revised Standard Version of the Bible and other translations include other versions of Mark's ending, we know that they were later additions and are not trustworthy. So Christians are left wondering why Mark ended his Gospel on such a note of mystery and suspense. It appears that Mark wants his readers to look outside the Gospel account for the presence of the risen Lord, in the church that is founded in his name, in their own hearts, in the ongoing mission that he helped organize (Acts 12:12, 25; 13:5; 15:39; Col. 4:10; Phlm. 24). Jesus may not appear directly in Mark's ending because the author wants readers to ask about Jesus' true identity and to keep on looking for him everywhere they go.

Matthew provides more information about what the resurrected Lord said and did. In the resurrection account itself he offers a brief dialogue. "Greetings" (called a *salutatio* or *salus*) was a common welcome in the Roman world similar to saying, "Hello," "*Bonjour*," or "*Guten tag*" in the modern world. Telling the disciples " 'Do not be afraid' " was a good idea, since they were distressed beyond words, wondering if it could possibly be true that Jesus was alive again, worrying about possible further persecution of the Romans, and having no idea what might happen next.

Luke and John have much more to report about the risen Jesus' encounters with his friends and followers. Luke's account of the walk to Emmaus and the discussion with Cleopas and another unnamed traveler (Luke 24:13–35) has no parallel in the other Gospels and relates that Jesus took the trouble to explain the meaning of his death and resurrection in the context of fulfillment of Old Testament texts, the blessing and breaking of bread (a precursor of the Lord's Supper?), and their eventual recognition of who he was. Their response to his presence is very moving: " 'Were not our hearts burning within us while he was walking with us on the road, while he was opening the scriptures to us?' " (v. 32).

In John's Gospel the tradition about what happened to Jesus after God raised him from the dead is dramatically expanded (John 20:11–31; 21:1–23). Since John's was the last Gospel to be written, we can see a definite progression from the most restricted and restrained comments about Jesus' raising in Mark's Gospel to detailed accounts in the Fourth Gospel of a quartet of appearances and three careful theological explanations of what these four events mean (20:30–31; 21:20–23; 21:24–25). The encounter with Mary provides a fascinating insight into what early believers expected to happen in their own faith. Mary, like many others, has her doubts that Jesus could possibly be alive, and when she sees him, she thinks he is the caretaker in the burial garden. It is only when he calls her by name that she recognizes him and throws herself upon him. Although she loves him, she cannot keep on hugging him, since he must ascend to the Father.

In John's second appearance story Jesus walks through a locked door (20:19–25) and breathes the Holy Spirit on the astonished disciples. Later, Thomas, in a well-known episode, denies the possibility that Jesus could really be alive and demands concrete evidence that what the disciples think they saw is verifiable. It is only when Jesus appears a third time (20:26–29) and orders Thomas to touch his mangled hands and wounded side that Thomas believes.

In John's fourth appearance narrative in chapter 21 (possibly added by another writer) Jesus speaks to his followers for the last time and meets them again in a familiar spot on the Sea of Galilee where they originally began their mission together. After showing them how they can catch more fish (and more followers) and having a "barbeque" with them, Jesus has a long discussion with Peter. In this exchange he reminds Peter of the fact that he denied him three different times and walks him through a confession by repeating the triple question " 'Do you love me?' " When Peter answers in the affirmative the final time, Jesus reminds all believers that the Christian faith is not ultimately about them as individuals but about the need to follow him in service to others. In this respect—that is, that the resurrection and new life lead to service—Matthew and John definitely agree.

An understanding of the resurrection for the first Christians is amplified by its use in other parts of the New Testament. In a critical passage in 1 Corinthians 15:4–8, for example, Paul testifies that Jesus' living presence was a certifiable historical event: he appeared to Peter after the third day, to the twelve disciples, to more than five hundred brothers and sisters at one time, to his brother James and the other apostles, and then, at the last, to Paul himself. As if responding to the doubts of some twenty-first-century Christians about the possibility that the resurrection could really have occurred, Paul asks them how they can say, "There is no resurrection of the dead." In his estimation, the fact that God raised Jesus from the dead is the core of Christian beliefs, and without it preaching and faith are both "in vain" and "futile" (15:12–19). This view still prevails in a document written much later when the author of 1 Peter announces that believers are given "a new birth into a living hope through the resurrection of Jesus Christ from the dead" (1 Pet. 1:3) and proclaims that it is a key factor in creating fundamental trust in the power of God (1:21).

Although modern Christians may struggle with historical questions about Jesus' resurrection and wonder if such a possibility can be verified scientifically, every reader of Matthew's Gospel must take his account seriously and come to terms with it. At the very end of his report Matthew clearly states his certainty of Easter's necessity: believers will only have a mission in their life and work if they encounter the living Christ, who commands them to go and is with them to the close of the age (28:20).

The Need for a Counternarrative (28:11–15)

Matthew records that denials concerning the veracity of the resurrection account surface immediately and are deliberately sown by Jesus' enemies. The chief priests and elders plot to concoct a consistent story that will be convincing in official quarters ("to the governor's ears") and to the public. After the guards (Gk., *custodias*) relate that the tomb is empty (did they see the angel too?), a plan is hatched to bribe the soldiers to get their accounts straight: " 'You must say, "His disciples came by night and stole him away while we were asleep" ' " (v. 13). This official approach is consistent with the way Matthew has portrayed the attitude of the religious leaders, King Herod, and Roman officials toward Jesus from the beginning. They were never interested in believing in him; they just wanted to deal with him and get him safely out the way. Modern believers may be reminded of contemporary attempts of public officials to "spin" the truth, deny charges of fraud and misconduct, and distract the public and journalists from close scrutiny of the facts.

In 28:15 Matthew abandons his role as a storyteller who is relating what happened to Jesus as it occurred and steps into the present time of his readers as the omniscient narrator. In this verse he brings the charge of subterfuge against Jesus' enemies and the opponents of the church up-to-date for his readers: "And this story is still told among the Jews to this day." It is a personal observation not about what happened in Jerusalem but what he is experiencing as he writes many years later.

Birth of the Church (28:16–20)

In Matthew's closing, as Jesus returns to the mountain in Galilee where so much revelation of God's truth had already occurred, the writer focuses on the creation of the church by the risen Christ. In this setting, where he has previously proclaimed the essence of the kingdom of heaven in the Sermon on the Mount (chapters 5–7) and has received God's endorsement at the transfiguration (17:1–8), Jesus now sends the eleven remaining disciples out with a command that will define and empower Christian mission for all the years since: " 'Go therefore and make disciples of all nations, baptizing them in the name of the Father and of the Son and of the Holy Spirit, and teaching them to do everything that I have commanded you. And remember, I am with you always, to the end of the age' " (v. 20).

Traditionally, this directive is called "the Great Commission" and refers to the authority given by Jesus to his disciples to preach, teach, and live the good news of the gospel all over the world and throughout the ages. This commissioning is reminiscent of Moses laying his hands on Joshua, installing him to be his successor (Num. 27:18–23); of Elijah's passing on of the prophetic cloak to his servant Elisha (1 Kgs. 19:19–21); and of the reception by Nehemiah and Ezra of royal commands to rebuild the city of Jerusalem. In Matthew more is involved than one person naming a successor, of course, since Jesus also gives the remaining eleven disciples the power of the Holy Spirit. He promises, what is more, that he will be with his disciples always, an extension of a powerful promise already made in 18:19–20: " 'Again, truly I tell you, if two or three of you agree on earth about anything you ask, it will be done for you by my Father in heaven. For where two or three are gathered in my name, I am there among them.' "

The Great Commission is also significant for another reason: it contains a clear Trinitarian statement. For centuries Christians have believed that God is one in three persons: Father, Son, and Holy Spirit. When this statement developed into a generally accepted doctrine is difficult to say, but by the fourth century CE it was widely expressed when the Nicene Creed was adopted by the church in 325 CE. Nevertheless, early versions of the Apostles' Creed already claimed faith in God the Father Almighty, Jesus Christ his only Son, and the Holy Spirit. Rudiments of this concept are also found in several New Testament texts (1 Thess. 1:1; Rom. 8:2; Gal. 1:3–5; 1 Cor. 1:18–2:5; 2:10; 2 Cor. 1:22; Phil.1: 6–11; Col. 1:15–20; also see John 1:1–14; Heb. 1:1–6). The significance of Matthew's final section is that the intimate connection between the Father, Son, and Holy Spirit is expressed by Jesus himself in his own words. Those who are suspicious about the history of this doctrine or struggle to understand and accept it need to study the concept of the Trinity in more detail and decide how they value the words attributed directly to Jesus at the end of Matthew's Gospel.

The final aspect of the Great Commission that is significant relates to the concept of evangelism, that is, the command to teach and preach the gospel throughout the world. This order has parallels in Luke 24:47–48 where the universal nature of the message of the kingdom is verified and in John 21 where Jesus directs Peter and the other disciples to "feed my sheep." The acceptance of this primary function of the church gave the apostles and later Christians the courage and power to go throughout the world to spread the good news about Jesus Christ. The faithful response to Jesus' commission led quickly to the establishment of Christian communities in Palestine, Syria, Lebanon, Egypt, Spain, and other parts of Europe. Many centuries later it became the watchword of the church's purpose in the late nineteenth and early twentieth centuries. During this period mission workers went to the Middle East, Africa, and the Far East in response to the goal of newly formed missionary societies in all the major denominations to go into all the world, "The Great Century of Mission"[1] as Michael Parker puts it. Between the years of 1859–1927, for example, the number of Presbyterian missionaries grew from 159 to a peak number of 2,159. Mission work grew in other churches with similar exponential growth. At the beginning of the twenty-first century a renewed commitment to worldwide Christian evangelism and service is reappearing, characterized by a heightened recognition in many denominations that a new "missional theology" and "missional structure" are needed that recognize that in times of cultural, political, military, and financial upheaval the purpose of the church of Jesus Christ is not just survival but the empowering and equipping of all believers in Jesus Christ. The challenge for Christians today is to obey the closing mandate in Matthew's Gospel in order to become God's messengers and servants to their own communities and to the whole world.

Notes

1. Michael Parker, "From Haystack to Historic, Celebrating a Dynamic Heritage of Overseas Mission," *Presbyterians Today* (May 2010): 19.

Part Two

LEADER'S GUIDE

DONALD L. GRIGGS

Guidelines for Bible Study Leaders

Goals of the Course

Even though one could read and study this course on the Gospel of Matthew without being a member of a class, the greatest value of the study will be realized when the reader is engaged with others who are companions on the journey. As I developed the Leader's Guide for this course, I had in mind several goals that I hoped the participants would experience as a result of their study. I expect that the participants will

- bring to their study a desire to enter more deeply into the world of the Bible and the world of the Gospel of Matthew.

- enjoy studying the Bible with others.

- come to a greater understanding and appreciation of the structure and message of the Gospel of Matthew.

- share their insights, questions, and affirmations with other study participants.

- develop a discipline of reading and studying the Bible on a regular basis.

Basic Teaching Principles

As I prepared these session plans I worked hard to implement a number of basic principles for effective teaching and leading. The foundational principle is an attempt to involve everyone in the class in as many activities as possible during every session every week. That's a big goal! It is not possible to succeed with everyone every week, but there are many opportunities for individuals to participate each week, and most will if they are encouraged to do so. You will see this principle present in all of the session plans that follow. I had at least a dozen other principles in mind as I designed this course:

- The leader serves best as companion and guide in the journey of the course.

- The leader provides sufficient information but not so much that participants lose the joy of discovery.

- Motivation for learning involves enjoying and completing tasks as well as making choices.

- Participants learn best when a variety of activities and resources are used in order to respond to their different interests, needs, and learning styles.

- Participants need to be invited to express their feelings, ideas, and beliefs in creative ways that are appropriate to them and to the subject matter.

- All participants need opportunities to share what they understand and believe.

- Open-ended questions invite interpretation, reflection, and application.

- Persons are nurtured in faith when they share their faith stories with one another.

- All teaching and learning happens in planned and unplanned ways and is for the purpose of increasing biblical literacy and faithful discipleship.

- The Bible becomes the living word of God when teachers and learners see their own faith stories expressed in Scripture.

- The Bible provides many resources to prompt our prayers, confessions of faith, and commitment to the ministry of Jesus Christ.

Room Arrangement

Arrange the room where you meet in such a way that participants are seated at tables. Tables are important because they provide space for all of the materials and the coffee cups. They also suggest that participants are going to work; they are not to just sit and listen to a lecture. If members of the group do not know everyone, then they all need name tags. Set up a table with hot water and makings for coffee, tea, and hot chocolate just inside the entrance to the room so everyone can get a cup and then find a seat. If you have a small group, arrange the tables in a rectangle or square so that everyone can see all the other members of the group. With a small group you will be able to be seated with them. On the other hand, if you have a large group, arrange the tables in a fan shape pointed toward the front so the participants can see the leader standing at the front of the group with a white board, newsprint easel, or bulletin board.

Resources

On the first week, be sure to provide Bibles for those who do not bring one. Continue to provide Bibles for those occasions when it is important for everyone to have the same translation and edition if you plan for them all to look at the same pages at the same time. However, encourage everyone to bring his or her own Bible. In addition to the Bibles, borrow from the church library, the pastor's library, and/or your own library copies of Bible dictionaries, Matthew commentaries, and Bible atlases. A church library will not ordinarily have enough Bible dictionaries for each person to have one with which to work. For those sessions where members are responsible for searching for information about a passage, person, or event in Matthew, make photocopies of the appropriate articles in a Bible dictionary, encyclopedia, or atlas. For one-time use, for one class, it is not a violation of the copyright laws.

Be sure to provide paper and pencils for those who don't bring them. Almost all of the activity sheets to be used by the participants are at the end of the respective session plans for which they will be used. There are several other activity sheets that will need to be reproduced for the participants.

Time

I planned each session to be an hour in length. If you have less than an hour, you will have to make some adjustments. It will be better to leave an activity out than to rush class members through all of the planned activities. Perhaps it would be possible in your situation to schedule more than seven sessions. There is probably enough material here for eight to ten sessions. If you had that much time, you would truly be able to deal with everything carefully, without hurrying.

If you find that members of your class have not already studied the first two books of this series, *The Bible from Scratch: The Old Testament for Beginners* or *The Bible from Scratch: The New Testament for Beginners* you may find it helpful to use session one from either of those courses, which provide a helpful orientation to the Bible and Bible study.

Final Word

As you prepare to teach this course, it is essential that you read each chapter of the Participant's Guide as you consider your teaching strategy for each session of the course. You should assume that many, though not all, of the participants will have read the respective chapter before coming to the class session, and you should be as familiar with the material as they are. Exploring the Gospel of Matthew with fellow pilgrims on the journey of faith will be for them and for you a challenging, inspiring, growing, and satisfying experience. May God bless you with many discoveries and much joy on this journey. If you and the members of your Bible study group have found this course to be helpful you may want to plan for the next course in the series, *Luke's Gospel from Scratch: The New Testament for Beginners*.

Session One

Family Tree, Birth, and Early Life of Jesus

A Study of Matthew 1:1–2:23

BEFORE THE SESSION

Focus of the Session

In this session we will get the course off to a good start by building community, focusing on some of the features of Matthew's Gospel, comparing Matthew's narrative of Jesus' birth with Luke's narrative, and exploring briefly the five prophecies in the first two chapters.

Advance Preparation

- Take the time to read the whole of the Gospel of Matthew. Try to do it in one sitting. This will help you gain a sense of the structure, flow, and key features of the Gospel.

- Read an introductory article or two about Matthew in a study Bible or Bible dictionary.

- Read articles in a Bible dictionary that deal with "prophecy in Matthew" and the concept of "incarnation."

- Gather several Bible study tools to share with the participants: a single-volume Bible commentary and a commentary on the Gospel of Matthew, a Gospel parallels book if one is available, a Bible dictionary, and one or more study Bibles.

- Prepare ahead of time a sheet of newsprint on which you have printed the response to the closing prayer, "O come to us, abide with us, our Lord Emmanuel!"

- Provide a few extra Bibles for those who forget to bring one.

Physical Arrangements

Reread the section of "Guidelines for Bible Study Leaders" that offers suggestions regarding room arrangement, resources and materials, and refreshments. You should have everything ready for the first session so that you can make a good first impression, especially for those who are new to Bible study.

Teaching Alternatives

The session plan that follows assumes a minimum of an hour for the study. If you have less than an hour then you will need to make some adjustments in the plan. You could consider several possibilities: 1) extend the session to two sessions, 2) if the members of the group already know each other fairly well, you could skip the building-community activity, or 3) eliminate the "Exploring Five Prophecies" activity.

DURING THE SESSION
Welcoming the Participants

You will feel more relaxed and ready for leading the session if you set up the refreshments and have everything ready before the first persons arrive. If you expect a large group, it will be helpful to have assistance from another person or two to take care of all the set-up arrangements. Ask the participants to sign in and make name tags for themselves. Greet each one by name and with a warm welcome. Check to see who needs to borrow a Bible and give them one. Also, encourage them to bring a Bible next week. If any of the participants do not already have a copy of this course book, you should give them one so they will have access to any of the references you will make to it during the session.

Introducing the Course

As you begin the session there are several points you will want to emphasize:

- This first session will introduce participants to the Gospel of Matthew and look more closely at chapters 1 and 2.

- The remaining six sessions will move sequentially through the Gospel.

- The session plans will not necessarily repeat what is in the Participant's Guide but will be based on that material and the related portions of Matthew.

- It is expected that participants will read the relevant chapter in the Participant's Guide in preparation for each session.

- All participants should bring a Bible to class, preferably a study Bible if they have access to one.

- There will be some presentation by the leader in each session, but most of the time the leader will be guiding the class members through a series of activities designed to engage them with the key Scriptures and main ideas of each session.

- There are no "dumb questions." All questions are appropriate. Encourage the participants to ask questions of the leader and the group.

- Everyone's insights, ideas, and affirmations will be received and respected. It is important to feel free to express what is in one's mind and heart.

After you have finished your introduction to the session, invite participants to begin their journey through the Gospel of Matthew by joining you in a brief prayer.

Opening Prayer

Introduce this activity by stating that in each session there will be an opening prayer that will be prompted by the text of the week's study of Matthew's Gospel. In this session we deal with Jesus' birth in Bethlehem. No matter what time of the year you are leading this course, begin the session by singing the first stanza of "O Little Town of Bethlehem." This should be familiar enough to everyone that the group can sing without accompaniment. After singing the first stanza, read the fourth stanza as the opening prayer.

> *O holy Child of Bethlehem, descend to us, we pray;*
> *Cast out our sin and enter in, be born in us today.*
> *We hear the Christmas angels the great glad tidings tell;*
> *O come to us, abide with us, our Lord Emmanuel!*[1]

Building Community among the Participants

In this first session it will be important to take a little time for persons to introduce themselves. Invite each person to share three things about himself: name, a memory of a particular Sunday school teacher (if someone did not attend Sunday school, she might share a memory of a favorite school teacher), and a favorite story about Jesus. Be sure to introduce yourself in this activity, perhaps even first in order to model what you have in mind. After all have introduced themselves, affirm the wonderful memories and favorite Jesus stories that were shared and emphasize that it is a great foundation on which to build for your study of the Gospel of Matthew.

Introducing Matthew's Gospel

Since most participants will probably not have read in preparation for this first session, it would be helpful to provide an overview of the key points made in the introduction in the Participant's Guide, pages 4 to 8. There are three possible ways you could summarize the five main topics of the introduction. One way is for you to prepare a presentation to cover the key points. A second way is to direct the participants to the above pages and "walk" them through the five sections by highlighting the key points in each. And the third way is to divide the class into five groups and assign each group one of the five sections. Provide time for them to read and to prepare to present the key points of their section. If time will be limited, you will probably want to choose one of the first two options, for the third way will take more time.

Comparing Two Birth Narratives

The author of the Participant's Guide made several statements regarding the differences between the birth narratives in Matthew's Gospel and in Luke's Gospel. In this activity the participants will have the opportunity to compare the two birth narratives in order to see how different they are. Guide this activity through the following steps:

- Direct the class members to the worksheet on page 80 of the Leader's Guide.

- Divide the class into two groups, and assign the Matthew passage to one group and the Luke passage to the other.

- Encourage persons to work in pairs, each member of the pair with the same passage.

- Provide about ten minutes for the pairs to answer the eight questions based on their passage. (Suggest that if they cannot find an answer for a question, just leave it blank.)

- Reassemble as a whole group, and work with one question at a time, receiving answers from both passages.

After sharing answers to all eight questions, spend a few minutes reflecting on two additional questions:

- What do you sense to be the unique emphasis or approach of Matthew to presenting the birth of Jesus?

- What, if anything, surprised you as you compared the two Gospels?

Exploring Five Prophecies

On page 11 of the Participant's Guide we read, "For the early Christians, when it could be demonstrated that an event had been previously envisioned by a prophet, it was clear to them that it was truly happening according to God's will." Before you engage the class members in this activity of exploring the five prophecies in Matthew 1 and 2, it would be helpful to provide a little background:

- Prophets are faithful believers who have been inspired by God with insights regarding what God's will is for the people of Israel.

- Prophets are very much "in tune" with what is happening in their world as well as what motivates the people to be either faithful or unfaithful to God's commands.

- Prophets do not so much predict the future but rather proclaim what they believe God intends for the people.

- Prophets warn that there will be consequences if the people do not live according to God's law and way.

- The hope for a messiah, a deliverer anointed by God, is present in the writings of several prophets.

- In this light, the writer of Matthew's Gospel makes connections between the prophets' messages and the miracle of the birth of Jesus the Messiah.

You will see on pages 81 and 82 a chart of five Matthew passages with the corresponding passages that are quoted from four prophets: Isaiah, Jeremiah, Micah, and Hosea. Direct the class members to the chart, and guide them through a review of the Matthew passages and the corresponding passages from four of the prophets. When you look at the passages from the prophets, take a couple of minutes with each to notice a little more of the context in which the passage appears. It will be helpful for you to consult a Bible commentary on Matthew and the study Bible notes associated with the five references to prophetic sayings so that you will be able to guide the class members through this activity.

Closing

Our opening prayer was based on the Christmas hymn "O Little Town of Bethlehem." The closing will be in the form of a litany, also based on the same hymn, using the last line of the fourth stanza as a response: "O come to us, abide with us, our Lord Emmanuel!" (Print this response on a sheet of newsprint or a white board so that all can see it.) Invite the participants to say in unison the response after you have read each of the following petitions:

- O God, inspire us as we study and meditate on your Holy Word.

- Walk with us as we seek to serve you by what we say and do each day.

- By your Spirit, empower us to speak your truth in difficult situations.

- Open our hearts to share your love with family, friends, and even our enemies.

- Where there is estrangement with others help us to be reconciled with them.

- May we be assured of your presence in good times as well as the troubling times.

AFTER THE SESSION

Encourage the participants to read chapter 2 in the Participant's Guide and Matthew 3:1–4:25 in preparation for the next class session.

Notes

1. Phillips Brooks, "O Little Town of Bethlehem," *The Presbyterian Hymnal* (Louisville, KY: Westminster/John Knox Press, 1990), 43.

Comparing Two Birth Narratives		
Matthew 1:18–2:15	**Questions to Answer**	**Luke 1:26–38; 2:1–20**
1.	An angel appeared to whom with what message?	1.
2.	Where are Joseph and Mary when the angel appears to them?	2.
3.	Who is the ruler in Israel at the time of Jesus' birth?	3.
4.	Who appears in Bethlehem to greet the child and his family?	4.
5.	What is the setting where they greet the child and his family?	5.
6.	What do the visitors bring to the child and his family?	6.
7.	What happens after the visitors leave?	7.
8.	By what names or titles is the child identified in this passage?	8.

Five Prophecies in Matthew 1 and 2	
Prophets Passages	**Matthew Passages**
Isaiah 7:14 "Look, the young woman is with child and shall bear a son, and shall name him Immanuel." *Context:* The prophet warns King Ahaz against an alliance with a foreign power and tells him he should rely on God, who will give a sign regardless of Ahaz's refusal to listen.	*Matthew 1:21–23a* "Look, the virgin shall conceive and bear a son, and they shall name him Emmanuel." *Context:* An angel of the Lord speaks to Joseph in a dream, declaring that Mary's pregnancy is to fulfill what had been spoken by the Lord through the prophet, Isaiah.
Micah 5:2 "But you, O Bethlehem of Ephrathah, who are one of the little clans of Judah, from you shall come forth for me one who is to rule in Israel." *Context:* Jerusalem is under siege. The prophet declares that help will come from the small town of Bethlehem, famous as David's birthplace.	*Matthew 2:6* "And, you, Bethlehem, in the land of Judah, are by no means least among the rulers of Judah; for from you shall come a ruler who is to shepherd Israel." *Context:* King Herod summons the chief priests to inquire where the Messiah was to be born, and they told him in Bethlehem of Judea.
Hosea 11:1 "When Israel was a child, I loved him, and out of Egypt I called my son." *Context:* The prophet uses the metaphor of parent and child to recall the period of Israel's time of their wilderness journey.	*Matthew 2:15* "Out of Egypt I have called my son." *Context:* An angel warned Joseph in a dream to flee to Egypt to save the child from Herod's vengeful wrath. Matthew declares that this was to fulfill what the Lord had spoken through the prophet.
Jeremiah 31:15 "A voice is heard in Ramah, lamentation and bitter weeping. Rachel is weeping for her children; she refuses to be comforted for her children, because they are no more." *Context:* Words of the Lord, through Jeremiah, at a time of great turmoil in Israel when the nation is about to be defeated and taken captive. This verse begins a poem of comfort and hope.	*Matthew 2:18* "A voice was heard in Ramah, wailing and loud lamentation, Rachel weeping for her children; she refused to be consoled, because they are no more." *Context:* Matthew states that the suffering of the parents at the death of their infant sons is a fulfillment of what had been spoken by Jeremiah. God's purposes will not be thwarted by the evil deeds against God's people, neither during the time of Jeremiah nor the time of Jesus' birth.

Five Prophecies in Matthew 1 and 2 *(continued)*	
Unknown Reference to Prophets *Context:* Biblical scholars suggest a possible Old Testament reference, Judges 13:5–7, with the reference to Nazirites as ones who are consecrated to God from birth for special service. This is, however, not a direct link or quote. Others have made a connection between Nazareth and Nazorean.	*Matthew 2:23* "He will be called a Nazorean." *Context:* After Herod died, an angel appeared to Joseph in a dream and told him to return with the child and Mary to the land of Israel. But Joseph was afraid of Herod's son, Archelaus, so he went to the region of Galilee to the town of Nazareth.

Session Two

Jesus' Ministry Begins

A Study of Matthew 3:1–4:25

BEFORE THE SESSION
Focus of the Session

In this session we will focus on two chapters that provide the background for setting the stage of Jesus' ministry. You will want to help the participants make connections between the words of Matthew and their faith journeys today.

Advance Preparation

- Read Matthew 3:1–4:25 and chapter 2 in the Participant's Guide.

- Prepare ahead of time a sheet of newsprint on which you have printed the words to the hymn "Spirit of the Living God."

- Read articles in a Bible dictionary that deal with "John the Baptist," "Pharisees," "Sadducees," and the concepts of "repent" and "repentance."

- Find in your denomination's official documents the section on the sacrament of baptism, and select several statements to share with the class. Also, find the questions that are asked of parents for baptism of infants and the questions asked of adult believers in your church.

- Prepare a sheet of newsprint with the response for the closing litany, *"Lord Jesus, empower us to follow you faithfully."*

- Provide a few extra Bibles for those who forget to bring one.

Teaching Alternatives

Depending on the amount of time you have for your class you may find that there is one too many activities for this session. If that is the case, you will have to decide which of the following activities you are going to eliminate.

DURING THE SESSION
Welcoming the Participants

Arrive at class early enough to set up the refreshments and have everything ready before the first persons arrive. If you used name tags in the first session, you will want to have them available again. Hopefully there will be a few persons show up who did not attend the first session. Be sure to welcome them warmly and assure them they will catch on quickly with the study of Matthew and will be able to participate easily. If they did not bring a Bible, be sure to give them one to use during the class and give them a copy of this course book.

Opening Prayer

Matthew writes that the Spirit of God is present in the baptism of Jesus as well as in his temptations in the wilderness. For the opening prayer, lead the class in singing the one verse of the hymn "Spirit of the Living God" or let them listen to a recording of that hymn. The words and tune are simple enough for the class to sing without accompaniment.

Introducing John the Baptist

Guide the group through Matthew 3:1–12 by calling attention to the following aspects of the narrative:

- Speak about "repent" and "repentance" as the act of turning from going in one direction in order to go in a new, different direction. From what might John be asking the people to repent?

- Refer to John's quote of the prophet Isaiah (40:3).

- Make the connection of the resemblance of John the Baptist to the prophet Elijah (2 Kgs. 1:8).

- Identify the Pharisees and Sadducees.

- Focus on the difference between John's baptizing with water and the one who is coming baptizing with the Holy Spirit.

- Conclude by discussing these two questions:

    What do you sense to be the significance of the role of John the Baptist?

    Who are persons who have "prepared the way" for you to come to faith in Jesus Christ?

Reflecting on Jesus' Baptism

There are two parts to this activity; reading and reflecting on the narrative and reflecting on our own baptisms and baptisms in our church. Guide the group through the following process:

- Ask three group members to read Matthew 3:13–17, each from a different version or translation. It would be good if one of the versions were a paraphrase. They should read slowly and with expression.

- Instruct the rest of the group to listen for a key word or phrase that "jumps out" for them.

- After each reading, invite the class members to speak out the words or phrases that jumped out for them in that reading.

- Continue by asking the question, What are some insights or questions that emerge for you from these five verses?

- Move to reflecting on baptism of Christians today by first inviting persons to share what baptism means for them as they observe baptisms in their congregation's worship life.

- Share a statement or two from your denomination's official foundational documents regarding the meaning and purpose of baptism.

- Read the questions that are asked of parents and/or believers as they present their children or themselves for baptism. As you read the questions for adult believers, invite the class members to answer the questions.

- Conclude by discussing the question, What does it mean to you that you have been baptized into the Christian faith community?

Exploring Jesus' Temptations

Guide the participants in exploring the narrative of Jesus' temptations by using the following process:

- Divide the group into three smaller groups. (If you have a large group, you could divide into six or nine groups of three or four persons each.)

- Direct the participants to page 89 of the Leader's Guide to the worksheet "Exploring the Temptations of Jesus."

- Each group will focus on one of the three temptations by reading their few verses and answering the five questions. (If they do not have access to a Bible with cross-references or a study Bible, you will need to direct them to the three passages from Deuteronomy from which Jesus quotes in his responses to Satan: Deut. 8:3; 6:16; and 6:13.)

- After about five minutes invite the participants to return to the large group and then spend a few minutes with the small groups reporting their answers to the first four questions.

- Next, spend a few minutes reflecting on the fifth question as you make a connection between this and the second question.

- Conclude with an additional question: Jesus quotes from Deuteronomy, which represents Moses' last words of instruction to the people of Israel before they entered the Promised Land. The 'wilderness' where Jesus is tempted is similar to the wilderness where Moses and the people are. What connections and/or similarities do you see between these wilderness experiences of Moses and Jesus?

Reflecting on the Beginning of Jesus' Ministry

Guide the class members to read through 4:12–25, in which there are a number of clues as to the nature of Jesus' ministry as he began. Lead them in this process:

- As they read through the passage, ask them to call out key words and phrases that are clues they see regarding the nature of Jesus' ministry. (Examples are "he left Nazareth," "made his home in Capernaum," "fulfilled the prophet," "proclaimed a message of repentance," and others.)

- After identifying these clues, lead a discussion of this question: Based on these fourteen verses what impressions or insights do you have regarding the nature of Jesus' ministry?

- Conclude by discussing one more question: What do you see as the relevance of the words "disciple" and "discipleship" for today's Christians?

Closing

Direct the participants to complete a sentence that begins "Jesus calls us to . . ." Give them a minute to complete the sentence and then invite them to share their sentences. In response to each sentence that is shared, the whole group will say in unison, "Lord Jesus, empower us to follow you faithfully."

AFTER THE SESSION

Encourage the participants to read chapter 3 in the Participant's Guide and Matthew 5:1–9:38 in preparation for the next class session.

Exploring the Temptations of Jesus

	First Temptation Matthew 4:3–4	Second Temptation Matthew 4:5–7	Third Temptation Matthew 4:8–10
1. What is the temptation?			
2. What does the temptation represent?			
3. What is Jesus' response?			
4. What is the source of the Scripture that Jesus quotes?			
5. In what ways are we or the church similarly tempted?			

Session Three

The Core of Jesus' Teaching and Healing

A Study of Matthew 5:1–9:38

BEFORE THE SESSION

Focus of the Session

In this session we will work through a lot of material in five chapters of Matthew's Gospel as we focus on the Beatitudes, Jesus' interpretation of the Law, four spiritual disciplines, and eight healing miracles of Jesus.

Advance Preparation

- Read Matthew 5:1–9:38 and chapter 3 in the Participant's Guide.

- Refer to a Bible commentary on Matthew as you prepare for this session, especially the section of the Beatitudes.

- Read articles in a Bible dictionary that deal with "Beatitudes," "Jesus' interpretation of the Law," and "miracles."

- Prepare ahead of time a sheet of newsprint on which you have printed the response in the closing litany prayer, "Abide with me Lord Jesus."

- Provide a few extra Bibles for those who forget to bring one.

Teaching Alternatives

Depending on the amount of time you have for your class, you may find that there is one too many activities for this session. If that is the case you will have to decide which of the following activities you are going to eliminate.

DURING THE SESSION
Welcoming the Participants

Arrive at class early enough to set up the refreshments and have everything ready before the first persons arrive. If you used name tags in the first two sessions, you will want to have them available again. Hopefully there will be a few persons show up that did not attend the first two sessions. Be sure they receive a warm welcome, and assure them they will catch on quickly with the study of Matthew and will be able to participate easily. If they did not bring a Bible, be sure to give them one to use during the class and give them a copy of this course book.

Opening Prayer: A Litany of Beatitudes

I have heard Archbishop Elias Chacour, a Palestinian Christian and author of *Blood Brothers*, speak often about his understanding of Jesus' teaching in the passage we know as the Beatitudes. When he read the text in Aramaic, the language Jesus spoke, the word translated as "blessed" is *ashre*, which he translates as "straighten up, go ahead, do something." This provides a different perspective or interpretation of the very familiar words. (If you have access to *The New Interpreter's Study Bible* check out the excursus (p. 754) on the Hebrew word *ashre*, where you will gain additional understanding of this concept.)

Direct the participants to the litany on page 96 of the Leader's Guide, and before praying, introduce it with the above paragraph. This litany is based on Archbishop Chacour's interpretation of the Beatitudes, with action expected of the ones to receive God's blessing.

Reflecting on the Beatitudes

There are nine blessings in Matthew 5:3–11. Take a few minutes to expand on the author's exposition of the Beatitudes on pages 22–23 of the Participant's Guide, based on your study and research using a commentary of Matthew and/ or a study Bible. Here are some points to make:

- The blessings were addressed to a community of believers, not necessarily individuals.

- The Beatitudes as words of Jesus were written by the author of the Gospel to address a community of believers living after the fall of Jerusalem in a period of persecution and uncertainty.

- The nine blessings are not Jesus' new rules for living; rather, they are declarations of what is experienced by believers in the present and what is hoped for in the future of God's kingdom.

- Each of the Beatitudes has two parts: part A speaks to a present reality ("Blessed are") while part B points toward an eschatological hope of the future ("for they will").

- Offer additional comments on each of the blessings from notes you gained by reading a commentary on this portion of Matthew's Gospel.

- Conclude with a brief discussion of two questions:

  What connections do you see between the litany with which we began the session and our discussion of the Beatitudes?

  What is the relevance of the Beatitudes for our faith today?

Considering Jesus' Sayings, "You have heard that it was said . . ."

In Matthew 5, there are six passages that begin with Jesus saying, "You have heard that it was said . . . but I say to you. . . ."

- Read in unison the introduction to those six passages, Matthew 5:17–20, which expresses Jesus' understanding of the place of the " 'law or the prophets.' "

- Then direct the participants to page 97 of the Leader's Guide where the six passages are listed with related passages from the Old Testament.

- Assign each pair of participants a different passage. (If you have more than twelve class members, you can either form triads or repeat the passages among additional pairs.) Ask each pair to read its assigned passage and the related Old Testament passage and then reflect on the question that follows the list of passages.

- Conclude by discussing briefly one more question: How would you summarize the main point Jesus was seeking to make with his interpretations of the Law?

Thinking about Jesus' Teaching on Spiritual Disciplines

The Sermon on the Mount continues with Jesus' teaching regarding the spiritual disciplines of giving alms, praying, fasting, and centering one's heart. No doubt the most familiar of the passages is the one on prayer that features what we know as the Lord's Prayer. After sharing some of your findings about these spiritual disciplines, spend a few minutes discussing two or more of the following questions:

- Jesus speaks of "practicing your piety." What is the meaning of *piety* for you? What might be a more contemporary synonym for *piety*?

- What connection, if any, do you see between the concept of piety and what we refer to as spiritual discipline?

- What are some experiences you have had with one or more of the four spiritual disciplines that Jesus addresses?

- What would be missing from our corporate weekly liturgies if the Lord's Prayer were omitted from the order of service?

- Martin Luther is believed to have said, "Prayer should be brief, frequent, and intense." How do you respond to that statement?

Exploring Healing Miracles of Jesus

In Matthew 8 and 9, there are nine brief passages, each featuring a healing miracle of Jesus. In the midst of these healing miracles are narratives of Jesus stilling the storm, Jesus calling Matthew to follow him, Jesus being questioned about his disciples not fasting, and a closing proclamation of Jesus: " 'The harvest is plentiful, but the laborers are few' " (9:37). In this activity we will focus on eight of the nine healing miracles. Lead the class in the following process:

- Direct them to the worksheet on page 98 of the Leader's Guide.

- Divide the class into eight small groups. (If you have fewer than sixteen in your class, eliminate one or more of the miracle narratives.)

- Each small group is to focus just on its assigned passage and answer the four questions based on their reading of that passage.

- After about five minutes of working in the small groups, reconvene as a total group.

- Work with one question at a time, asking each of the groups to share its answers.

After all the passages and answers have been shared, spend a few minutes discussing one or more of the following questions:

- What do you discern to be Matthew's approach to presenting the good news about Jesus?

- What have you learned about the nature of Jesus' ministry in terms of the types of persons he responds to and the ways he conducts himself?

- Read 9:35–38. How do you interpret this passage as it concludes this section of Matthew's Gospel?

- What clues do you see, if any, regarding our approach to ministry in Jesus' name today?

Closing

This session's closing prayer is in the form of a litany. As leader, read each of the following sayings of Jesus and instruct the participants to respond in unison, "Abide with me. Lord Jesus." Repeat the response a couple of times, inviting the participants to say it with you so they will be able to respond without hesitation after each saying of Jesus.

- Jesus said, " 'You are the salt of the earth' " (5:13).

- Jesus said, " 'You are the light of the world' " (5:14).

- Jesus said, " 'Beware of practicing your piety before others in order to be seen by them' " (6:1).

- Jesus said, " 'When you are praying, do not heap up empty phrases' " (6:7).

- Jesus said, " 'Do not store up for yourselves treasures on earth' " (6:19).

- Jesus said, " 'Do not worry about your life, what you will eat or . . . what you will wear' " (6:25).

AFTER THE SESSION

Encourage the participants to read chapter 4 in the Participant's Guide and Matthew 10:1–13:58 in preparation for the next class session.

Straighten Up, You Faithful of God

(Based on Matthew 5:1–12)

God calls you to get up and move, you who are poor in spirit, for yours is the kingdom of heaven.

> *I desire to be with you, God; you are my strength and my life.*

Straighten up, you people who grieve, for you will be comforted.

> *I seek your comfort and love in my time of sorrow and despair.*

Lift up your head, you who are humble, for you will inherit the earth.

> *O God, help me to know my place of worth in your realm.*

Set yourself in a new direction, you who hunger and thirst for righteousness, for you will be filled.

> *You grant me more than I deserve, and I am deeply grateful, gracious God.*

When you do acts of mercy, you will receive mercy.

> *Remind me, O God, that I am to show compassion for the other, as you do.*

When you act as persons whose hearts are pure, you shall see God.

> *I am unworthy, and yet you receive me into your presence.*

Commit yourself to be a peacemaker, not a peace contemplator. Then you will be called children of God.

> *I believe that to be your child is to work for peace among ALL your children.*

Do the right thing, and then the kingdom of heaven will be yours.

> *You welcome me into your realm, which is more important than anything I could expect.*

You are to act with courage and integrity in response to those who insult you, mistreat you, and tell evil lies about you because of your faith in Jesus Christ.

> *Be with me, my God, as I seek to be a faithful witness to your peace, your love, and your justice. AMEN*

Jesus' Interpretation of the Law

Matt. 5:21–26	Murder (see Exod. 20:13)
Matt. 5:27–30	Adultery (see Exod. 20:14)
Matt. 5:31–32	Divorce (see Deut. 24:1–4)
Matt. 5:33–37	Swearing falsely (see Exod. 20:7)
Matt. 5:38–42	Revenge (see Exod. 21:24)
Matt. 5:43–48	Love of enemies (see Lev.19:18)

Question:
In each passage Jesus focuses on one of the traditional laws familiar to the people he was addressing. In what way does he expand on, underscore, or reinterpret the law from the Hebrew Scriptures?

Exploring Healing Miracles of Jesus				
	What was the motivation or circumstance of the healing?	How was the healing accomplished?	What was the response of the one(s) healed?	What were the responses of those who observed the healing?
1. Leper (8:1–4)				
2. Centurion's servant (8:5–13)				
3. Two Gadarene demoniacs (8:28–34)				
4. Paralytic (9:2–8)				
5. Young girl (9:18–19 and 23–26)				
6. Woman (9:20–22)				
7. Two blind men (9:27–31)				
8. Mute demoniac (9:32–34)				

Session Four
Expanded Urban Mission

A Study of Matthew 10:1–13:58

BEFORE THE SESSION
Focus of the Session

One of the key concepts we will focus on in this session is "discipleship." Jesus challenged his disciples, and challenges us, to act in ways that show they/we are being faithful in their/our discipleship. We will also deal with Jesus' encounters with the Pharisees and explore the parables found in chapter 13.

Advance Preparation

- Read Matthew 10:1–13:58 and chapter 4 in the Participant's Guide.

- Read articles in a Bible dictionary that deal with "Sabbath," "Pharisees," "parables," "Beelzebul," and "kingdom of heaven."

- If you can obtain a copy of Dietrich Bonhoeffer's book *The Cost of Discipleship*,[1] it would be good to find and read the quotes regarding "cheap grace" and "costly grace" directly from the book (see p. 101 below).

- Prepare ahead of time a sheet of newsprint on which you have printed "Equip us, God, to be Jesus' faithful followers," which is the litany response in the closing prayer.

- Provide a few extra Bibles for those who forget to bring one.

Teaching Alternatives

As with other sessions, you may find that there is one activity too many for the time you have for this session. If you need to omit an activity, you may consider doing just one of the parable activities.

DURING THE SESSION
Opening Prayer

Lead the class in the following prayer, or one that you have prepared, that focuses on this matter of being called as disciples of Jesus.

> *Calling God, we read of Jesus calling and empowering his first disciples, and we know that he is calling us to be his disciples today. Help us to understand what it means*
>
> > *to proclaim the good news,*
> > *to cure the sick and cleanse the lepers,*
> > *to be wise as serpents and innocent as doves,*
> > *and to lose our lives for Jesus' sake in order to find them.*
>
> *We pray in all sincerity that you will empower us and lead us as we seek to follow wherever Jesus will lead us. AMEN*

Reflecting on the Cost of Discipleship

Guide the class members in a process of reflecting on discipleship by doing the following:

- Assign half of the class to read Matthew 10:5–25, and the other half to read 10:26–39.

- As they read, they are to look for words of Jesus that indicate what he expects of his disciples and what the disciples can expect when they follow him.

- After providing time for reading, invite the participants to share what they found. Write their responses on newsprint or a white board in two columns: 1) What Jesus expects of his disciples and 2) What the disciples can expect to experience.

- After creating the two lists, introduce Dietrich Bonhoeffer as the German theologian who in 1937 during the rise of the Nazi regime wrote the book *The Cost of Discipleship* in which he contrasts cheap grace with costly grace.

- Read the following quotes from that book.

Cheap grace is the preaching of forgiveness without requiring repentance, baptism without church discipline, communion without confession, absolution without personal confession. Cheap grace is grace without discipleship, grace without the cross, grace without Jesus Christ, living and incarnate.[2]

Costly grace confronts us as a gracious call to follow Jesus; it comes as a word of forgiveness to the broken spirit and the contrite heart. It is costly because it costs [one his or her] life, and it is grace because it gives [one] the only true life. It is costly because it compels a [person] to submit to the yoke of Christ and follow him; it is grace because Jesus says: "My yoke is easy and my burden is light."[3]

Conclude this activity with a brief discussion of one or two questions:

- What are some connections you would make between Jesus' call to discipleship and Bonhoeffer's description of "cheap grace" and "costly grace"?

- What do you find challenging in Jesus' call to discipleship?

- What do you find hopeful in Jesus' call?

- What are the relevance of Jesus' call and Bonhoeffer's words for us today?

Considering Jesus and the Pharisees

In Matthew 12 there are four encounters between Jesus and the Pharisees. The issues include working on the Sabbath (v. 2), healing on the Sabbath (v. 14), Jesus' being identified with Beelzebul (v. 24), and Pharisees' seeking a sign from Jesus (v. 38). Make a brief presentation that will include the following information:

- A description of the Pharisees

- Examples of Sabbath laws

- A statement of who Beelzebul was

- Some reasons for the Pharisees' opposition to Jesus

- Jesus' responses to the accusations of the Pharisees

After making your brief presentation, follow up with discussion of a question or two such as those that follow or ones you have prepared.

- How would you characterize Jesus' encounters with the Pharisees?

- Jesus said earlier in Matthew that he came " 'not to abolish the law and the prophets but to fulfill them' " (5:17). In what ways do you think Jesus is attempting to fulfill the law regarding Sabbath observance?

- What can we learn from Jesus' understanding of the law and his relationship with religious authorities that has relevance for faith and life today?

- In what ways is Jesus modeling what he said earlier he expects of his disciples?

Reviewing the Parable of the Sower

A key feature of Jesus' teaching ministry was the use of parables. Matthew 13 begins with Jesus teaching crowds by the sea with a parable about a sower and four kinds of soil. Matthew then moves to Jesus' telling his disciples why he teaches in parables, followed by his explaining the meaning of the parable of the Sower. Include the following in a brief introduction:

- Jesus' use of parables as a major teaching strategy

- A definition of *parable* compared to *metaphor*, *simile*, and *allegory*

- The parable of the Sower and its explanation are presented in all three Synoptic Gospels

- An explanation that parables are not intended to be fully understood by all the hearers

Move to review the parable of the Sower, which might more appropriately be called the parable of the Four Soils. Engage the class members in the following way:

- Ask the class to count off by fours.

- Assign each number one of the four different "soils' roles": path, rocky ground, thorns, and good soil.

- Read the script on page 105 in the Leader's Guide, with the persons assigned to each soil role reading the appropriate lines.

- Then, turn to Matthew 13:18–23 where Jesus explains the parable to his disciples.

- Ask each of the "soils" to read the verse(s) associated with their role so that they will know what happens to the seed of the good news when it is spread on their soil.

- Tell the class members to stay in their soil role as they listen to a portion of the good news of Jesus' message. (What you are seeking to do is to help the participants to "hear" from the perspective of their "soil" and to describe what happens to the seed of the "good news" after it has been scattered on their soil.)

- Read Matthew 6:5–8, Jesus' teaching about prayer.

- Follow up with the question, What happened to the seed of the good news after it was received by your soil?

- Conclude with one more question: What are some examples of how the good news is spread, received, and responded to in our world today?

Exploring Six Parables

There are six more parables in Matthew 13. Each one is introduced with the phrase "The kingdom of heaven is like . . ." After you provide a brief explanation of the concept of "kingdom of heaven" as it appears in Matthew, lead the class through the following steps:

- Form six small groups. (If there are fewer than twelve class members, omit one or more of the parables.)

- Ask the participants to turn to page 105 of the Leader's Guide to find the worksheet "Exploring Six Parables in Matthew 13."

- Assign each group one of the parables.

- Ask each group to read its brief passage and then discuss the question that follows the list of six parables.

- After about ten minutes reconvene the whole group and invite participants to share some of their ideas that were discussed in the small groups.

- Conclude this activity by discussing another question: Jesus used objects and experiences from the culture of his day as the subjects of his parables. What are some objects and experiences from our day that might serve as a basis for saying, "The kingdom of heaven is like . . ."?

Closing

Conclude by inviting the participants to complete a sentence that begins with the phrase "Jesus teaches us to . . ." Give them a minute to think or write a completion to the unfinished sentence. Then, invite those who are willing to share their completed sentences. After each has spoken, the rest of the group will respond in unison, "Equip us, God, to be Jesus' faithful followers."

AFTER THE SESSION

Encourage the participants to read chapter 5 in the Participant's Guide and Matthew 14:1–20:34 in preparation for the next class session.

Notes

1. Dietrich Bonhoeffer, *The Cost of Discipleship* (New York: The Macmillan Company, 1949).
2. Ibid., 36.
3. Ibid., 37.

The Parable of the Sower and Four Soils (Matthew 13:1–9)

Introduction	That same day Jesus went out of the house and sat beside the sea. Such great crowds gathered around him that he got into a boat and sat there, while the whole crowd stood on the beach. And he told them many things in parables, saying: "Listen! A sower went out to sow.
The Path	"And as he sowed, some seeds fell on the path, and the birds came and ate them up.
Rocky Ground	"Other seeds fell on rocky ground, where they did not have much soil, and they sprang up quickly, since they had no depth of soil. But when the sun rose, they were scorched; and since they had no root, they withered away.
Thorns	"Other seeds fell among thorns, and the thorns grew up and choked them.
Good Soil	"Other seeds fell on good soil and brought forth grain, some a hundredfold, some sixty, some thirty.
Conclusion	"Let anyone with ears listen!"

Exploring Six Parables in Matthew 13

1. Parable of the Weeds	Matt. 13:24–30
2. Parable of the Mustard Seed	Matt. 13:31–32
3. Parable of the Yeast	Matt. 13:33
4. Parable of the Hidden Treasure	Matt. 13:44
5. Parable of the Fine Pearl	Matt. 13:45–46
6. Parable of the Net	Matt. 13:47–50

Question:
In what way does your parable offer a glimpse of the meaning of the kingdom of heaven?

Session Five

Prelude to Jerusalem

A Study of Matthew 14:1–20:34

BEFORE THE SESSION
Focus of the Session

Chapter 5 presents a lot of material summarizing these seven chapters of Matthew, which is more than we will have time for in this session. We will not be able to consider John the Baptist, all of the miracles performed by Jesus (we focused on miracles in session 3), his encounters with the Pharisees and Sadducees (we dealt with Pharisees in session 4), and his predictions about his death. We will focus on several key aspects of these seven chapters: the feeding of the five thousand, Peter's role in several narratives, and two parables.

Advance Preparation

- Read Matthew 14:1–20:34 and chapter 5 in the Participant's Guide.

- Refer to your notes from last session's preparation on the topics of "parables" and "kingdom of heaven."

- Read articles in a Bible dictionary that deal with "Messiah," "transfiguration," and "forgiveness."

- Consult a commentary on Matthew to be especially prepared to deal with the narratives on the feeding of the five thousand, the transfiguration, the parable of the Unforgiving Servant, and the parable of the Laborers in the Vineyard.

- Choose a hymn to sing as the closing, and print the words of the hymn if you want the class to sing more than the first stanza.

- Provide a few extra Bibles for those who forget to bring one.

DURING THE SESSION
Opening Prayer

We used this litany format in the closing of session 3. Speak the following sayings of Jesus and invite the class members to respond in unison after each saying, "Help me, Lord Jesus."

- Jesus said, " 'If any want to be my followers, let them deny themselves and take up their cross and follow me' " (16:24).

- Jesus said, " 'Whoever becomes humble like this child is the greatest in the kingdom of heaven. Whoever welcomes one such child in my name welcomes me' " (18:4–5).

- Jesus said, " 'Let the little children come to me, and do not stop them; for it is to such as these that the kingdom of heaven belongs' " (19:14).

- In response to the disciples' question " 'Who can be saved?' " Jesus said, " 'For mortals it is impossible, but for God all things are possible' " (19:25–26).

- Jesus said, " 'Everyone who has left houses or brothers or sisters or father or mother or children or fields for my sake, will receive a hundredfold, and will inherit eternal life' " (19:29).

Reflecting on the Feeding of the Five Thousand

The author of the Participant's Guide suggests that when the intended audience of Matthew's Gospel heard or read the narrative of the feeding of the five thousand, they would likely be reminded of God's action in the past (feeding the Israelites with manna in their desert journey from Egypt) and of Jesus' action at the Last Supper (the blessing and breaking of bread), which they remembered and celebrated weekly in their worship gatherings. After you or someone in the class has read aloud Matthew 14:13–21, take a few minutes to look closely at the text and discuss a question or two. As you review the text, be sure to call attention to the following points:

- The text begins "Now when Jesus heard this, he withdrew from there. . . ." What Jesus heard was the news of the death of John the Baptist (see Matt. 14:1–12).

- He withdrew in a boat by himself to a deserted place. Was this for Jesus a time of grieving and remembering?

- Crowds would not let Jesus grieve in peace; they followed him until he came ashore.

- Even in a time when Jesus wanted to be alone, he showed compassion by healing the sick.

- The disciples appear. Where did they come from? Did they walk with the crowd, or were they with him in the boat?

- The disciples wanted to send the crowds home. When Jesus told the disciples to feed the multitude, they responded that all they had were five loaves and two fish, which they gave to Jesus.

- Jesus blessed and broke the bread and gave it to the disciples, who distributed bread and fish until all ate and were filled, and there were twelve baskets full left over.

- Women and children were present, but only the men were counted, which means more than five thousand were fed.

Reflect on the narrative by guiding a discussion prompted by several questions such as these or ones that you have created:

- What connections do you see between this feeding by Jesus and both God's feeding the Israelites with manna in the wilderness and Jesus' feeding the disciples with bread at the Last Supper?

- What do we learn about Jesus, the disciples, and the crowds from this narrative?

- What are some reasons that we might want to remember this feeding of the five thousand when we celebrate Holy Communion in our congregational worship?

- What is one question you have about this narrative?

- What is one truth you will take from this narrative?

Reviewing Peter's Role in Six Narratives

The disciple Peter is named twenty-three times in Matthew's Gospel; thirteen times in these seven chapters, eight times in chapter 26 on the occasion of Jesus' arrest, plus when the four fishermen are called by Jesus to follow him (4:18) and when the twelve disciples are named (10:2). In these seven chapters Peter is present six times:

1. when he tries to walk on the water (14:28, 29)

2. when he asks Jesus to explain a parable (15:15)

3. when Jesus and the disciples are in Caesarea Philippi where Peter speaks on their behalf, declaring Jesus as the Messiah (16:16)

4. when Jesus' transfiguration occurs (17:1, 4)

5. when he asks Jesus about how many times he should forgive (18:21)

6. when a rich young man decided he could not follow Jesus (19:27)

Involve the class members in a review of these six narratives, guided by the following process:

- Ask the class members to count off by sixes. (If there are fewer than twelve in your class, omit one or more of the narratives.)

- Assign each person one of the six Peter narratives. (See worksheet on page 112 of the Leader's Guide.)

- Instruct the participants to pair up with someone who is assigned the same narrative.

- Their task is to read the passage and answer the three questions. This should take only five to seven minutes.

- After giving them time to answer the three questions, direct the class members to form new groups of three or four persons, each person with a *different* narrative to share.

- When the new groups of three or four are formed, give these instructions: "In this activity you are going to use your spirit-led imaginations. Imagine yourself in the role of Peter; put his sandals on your feet and speak as if you are Peter. Speak to the others in your small group about three things: 1) the occasion of the event, 2) your motivations as Peter for your involvement, and 3) your impressions of or questions about Jesus." (Remind them to share short, not long, stories.)

- Provide about ten minutes for the sharing, and then call the groups to return to the whole class.

Conclude this activity with a brief discussion guided by a question or two:

- What insights have come to you about the ministry of Jesus?

- What are some ways that you identify with Peter?

- What relevance do you see between Peter's "walk" with Jesus and our walk in faith with him today?

Exploring Two Parables

There are two extended parables in this section of Matthew: the parable of the Unforgiving Servant (18:23–35) and the parable of the Laborers in the Vineyard (20:1–16). As in chapter 13, these two parables are also introduced with the phrase "The kingdom of heaven may be compared to . . ." or "is like . . ."

- In order to explore the two parables the class members need to be formed into small groups again. An easy way to accomplish this is to ask them to return to the small groups of three or four that they were in for the previous activity.

- Assign half of the small groups one parable and the other half the second parable.

- The task of each group is to read the parable and then to discuss the question, What does this parable teach us about the kingdom of heaven?

- After ten to fifteen minutes ask the groups to reconvene with the whole group and spend some time sharing their responses.

- Conclude with discussion of an additional question: What can we take from this teaching of Jesus to apply to our faith journeys today?

Closing

Close your session by inviting the class to sing the first stanza of a familiar hymn. If you have hymnals available or decide to make copies of the words, it would be great to sing all the stanzas, if time permits. Here are some hymns you might consider, or choose another that you feel is appropriate:

"O Master, Let Me Walk with Thee"

"O Jesus I Have Promised"

"Christ of the Upward Way"

"Lord, I Want to Be a Christian"

AFTER THE SESSION

Encourage the participants to read chapter 6 in the Participant's Guide and Matthew 22:1–27:66 in preparation for the next class session.

Reviewing Peter's Role in Six Narratives

Instructions: You will be assigned one of the following six narratives in which Peter is a key character. Pair up with another person who is assigned the same passage. Read the passage and then answer the three questions below.

14:22–33	Peter tries to walk on water.
15:10–20	Peter asks Jesus to explain a parable.
16:13–20	Peter identifies Jesus as the Messiah.
17:1–13	Peter and John accompany Jesus to a high mountain.
18:21–35	Peter asks Jesus how many times he must forgive.
19:16–30	Peter observes Jesus' encounter with a rich young man.

Questions:

1. What is the occasion of the encounter between Peter and Jesus?

   _____

   _____

2. What do you think Peter understands or does not understand regarding Jesus?

   _____

   _____

3. What impressions or questions might Peter have had of Jesus?

   _____

   _____

Session Six

The Messiah in God's City

A Study of Matthew 21:1–27:66

BEFORE THE SESSION

Focus of the Session

There is a great amount of material in chapters 21 through 27 of Matthew. The focus for the session will be on Jesus' entry into Jerusalem and the events of the second day, on a central point of Jesus' teaching regarding the great commandment, and on twelve events that occurred during Jesus' last few days in Jerusalem.

Advance Preparation

- Read Matthew 21:1–27:66 and chapter 6 in the Participant's Guide.

- Consult a Matthew commentary and/or notes in a study Bible related to 21:1–27 in order to prepare for your presentation on the four narratives in that chapter.

- Read articles in a Bible dictionary that deal with "Passover," "Caiaphas," "Pilate," and "crucifixion."

- Try to find a map showing Jerusalem in the time of Jesus where you can identify locations of the temple, Garden of Gethsemane, Mount of Olives, and so on.

- If you would like to have words for the closing hymn, "Were You There?" you may want to arrange for some hymnals or to print the words of the four stanzas on a sheet of newsprint.

- Provide a few extra Bibles for those who forget to bring one.

DURING THE SESSION
Opening Prayer

We read in Matthew's Gospel that when Jesus was on the road to Jerusalem, the people welcomed him with an acclamation of " 'Blessed is the one who comes in the name of the Lord!' " (21:9). The author of the Participant's Guide writes that there was an "echo of the words of thanksgiving to God in Psalm 118:26" (p. 48). Selected verses of this psalm are the basis for our opening prayer. Direct the class members to page 118 of the Leader's Guide for "An Antiphonal Reading of Psalm 118." For the opening prayer, divide the group into two sections, with one reading the lines in plain font and the other reading the lines in italics.

Considering Jesus' Entry and First Days in Jerusalem

As a result of reading a Matthew commentary and notes in a study Bible, you will be prepared to lead the class in their consideration of Matthew 21:1–27, which includes four narratives. Focus on each, one at a time, with a brief presentation and reflection.

1. Jesus' Entry into Jerusalem (21:1–11)

- If you have access to a map, show the locations of the Mount of Olives and the Temple in the Old City of Jerusalem.

- Make connections to Zechariah 9:9 and Psalm 118:25.

- Review the meaning of the expression "Hosanna to the Son of David."

- Point out the significance of Jesus' riding on a beast of burden.

2. Jesus Cleanses the Temple (21:12–17)

- Try to find a teaching print of the Temple at the time of Jesus from the Sunday school collection or some other resource.

- Identify the key characters in the drama of this passage with a few comments about each: money changers, the blind and lame, chief priests and scribes, and children.

- Review the practice of exchanging money in order to purchase animals for the sacrifice ritual.

- Make connections with Isaiah 56:7, Jeremiah 7:11, and Psalm 8:2.

3. Jesus Curses a Fig Tree (21:18–22)

- This passage is more likely a symbolic story than the report of a historical event.

- Refer to Isaiah 34:4 and Jeremiah 8:12–13, where the fig tree and its fruit are compared to an unfaithful Israel.

- Remind everyone that Matthew was written after the destruction of the Temple in 70 CE.

4. Jesus' Authority Is Questioned (21:23–27)

- This is the next day when Jesus enters the Temple a second time.

- Notice that Jesus is teaching in the Temple.

- Look carefully at the exchange of questions and answers between Jesus and the religious leaders.

Conclude by spending a few minutes discussing the following question or a question you have planned: What have we learned about the nature of Jesus' life and ministry from these four brief passages?

Thinking about Jesus' Teachings in His Last Days

In Matthew 21:28–22:46 and 25:1–30 we read of five parables and four issues about which the religious leaders questioned Jesus. In order to leave time for the activity that follows it would be best to mention only these parables and issues. However, it would be good to focus on the most central of Jesus' teachings as he responded to the Pharisees and Sadducees who asked, " 'Which commandment in the law is the greatest?' " (22:36). Take time to do the following:

- Divide the class into three sections.

- Assign each section a different one of the following passages: Matthew 22:34–40; Mark 12:28–34; and Luke 10:25–30.

- Ask them to turn to their assigned passage and to look for answers to the questions that follow.

- Present one question at a time, and invite answers from each section based on what they read in their passage.

    Question 1: Who asked Jesus a question about the law?

    Question 2: What was the motivation for asking the question?

    Question 3: What was Jesus' response to the question or questioner?

    Question 4: What was the follow-up response of the one who asked the question?

    Question 5: What are the references in the Hebrew Scriptures that are quoted?

The purpose of this exercise is to help the class members see that there are significant differences between the three Synoptic Gospels regarding this narrative. You should complete this exercise ahead of time so that you will know the answers to each question from each Gospel. (The references to answer question 5 are Deut. 6:4 and Lev. 19:18.) Conclude by reflecting on one more question: What is the significance of this teaching of Jesus and the Hebrew Scriptures for our faith and life today?

Retelling Twelve Events of Jesus' Last Days

There are twelve episodes in chapters 26 and 27. That is a lot of material to cover in twenty to twenty-five minutes. Lead the activity through the following process:

- Direct the class members to page 119 in the Leader's Guide.

- Assign each person a different passage. (If there are fewer than twelve, omit one or more episodes. If there are more than twelve, assign the same passage to two persons.)

- Ask each person to read his or her passage and to identify with one of the key characters in the event, but not Jesus. As they read, they are to imagine themselves present at the event. (This is similar to last week's activity related to the disciple Peter.)

- Alert them that after a few minutes for the reading they will be invited to retell the event in their own words, telling the story from the perspective of one who was present.

- Take the time necessary for the retelling of these events in Matthew 26 and 27. (Where two persons have read the same passage, ask them to each retell just a part of the narrative.) After retelling the narratives, ask the group to reflect on one or more questions:

    How did it feel to be part of the story?

    What are some of your impressions of Jesus from the perspective of the person you identified with?

    When you reflect on the present, what relevance is there to these views of Jesus to faith and life today?

Closing

An appropriate hymn to sing as the closing of the session is the African-American spiritual "Were You There?" This should be familiar enough to everyone that they can sing a cappella. The four verses are as follows:

Were you there when they crucified my Lord?
Were you there when they nailed Him to the tree?
Were you there when they pierced Him in the side?
Were you there when they laid Him in the tomb?[1]

AFTER THE SESSION

Encourage the participants to read chapter 7 in the Participant's Guide and Matthew 28:1–20 in preparation for the next class session.

Notes

1. "Were You There?" *The Presbyterian Hymnal* (Louisville, KY: Westminster/ John Knox Press, 1990), 102.

An Antiphonal Reading of Psalm 118

(Selected Verses)

O give thanks to the LORD, for he is good;

his steadfast love endures forever!

Out of my distress I called on the LORD;

the LORD answered me and set me in a broad place.

With the LORD on my side I do not fear.

What can mortals do to me?

It is better to take refuge in the LORD

than to put confidence in mortals.

The LORD is my strength and my might;

he has become my salvation.

This is the day that the LORD has made;

let us rejoice and be glad in it.

Blessed is the one who comes in the name of the LORD.

We bless you from the house of the LORD.

You are my God, and I will give thanks to you;

you are my God, I will extol you.

O give thanks to the LORD, for he is good,

for his steadfast love endures forever.

Retelling Twelve Events of Jesus' Last Days

Instructions: Read your assigned passage and, using your imagination, place yourself in the narrative as one who was present as a witness to the event.

26:6–13	Jesus anointed at Bethany
26:17–30	Jesus sharing Passover with his disciples
26:36–46	Jesus prays in Gethsemane
26:47–56	Jesus betrayed and arrested
26:57–68	Jesus before the high priest
26:69–75	Peter denies Jesus
27:1–10	Judas commits suicide
27:11–23	Jesus before Pilate
27:24–31	Jesus handed over to the soldiers
27:32–44	The crucifixion of Jesus
27:45–56	The death of Jesus
27:57–66	The burial of Jesus

Questions:

1. From the witness you have chosen to identify with, what is your role in the event?

_____

_____

2. What are some thoughts and feelings you have about what happened?

_____

_____

3. What will be the main thing you will remember about what happened in this
   event?

_____

_____

Resurrection and the Birth of the Church

A Study of Matthew 28:1–20

BEFORE THE SESSION

Focus of the Session

In this session we will focus on the last chapter of Matthew's Gospel that features the resurrection of Jesus, his appearance to the women, and the commissioning of the disciples. We will focus on the concept of resurrection, compare the resurrection narratives in all four Gospels, and also look at the doctrine of the Trinity. In addition, there will be a brief evaluation of the course and a closing with a charge to the whole class based on the Great Commission.

Advance Preparation

- Read Matthew 28:1–20 and chapter 7 in the Participant's Guide.

- Consult a Matthew commentary and/or notes in a study Bible related to 28:1–20.

- Read articles in a Bible dictionary that deal with "resurrection" and "Trinity."

- If you would like to have words for an opening hymn, you may want to arrange for some hymnals or to print the words on a sheet of newsprint.

- If you decide to recite the Apostles' Creed, you may want to prepare copies so that everyone will be able to participate.

- Prepare one or more newsprint sheets with the words of the responses by the class members for the closing commissioning.

- Provide a few extra Bibles for those who forget to bring one.

DURING THE SESSION
Opening Prayer

Since the focus of this session is the resurrection and appearances of Jesus, a good way to begin the session would be to sing a familiar Easter hymn. Choose a hymn that you know is familiar to your class, or choose from the following: "Christ the Lord Is Risen Today," "Jesus Christ Is Risen Today," "Thine Is the Glory," or "Celebrate with Joy and Singing." After singing one or more stanzas of the hymn, offer a brief prayer of praise and thanksgiving to God for the incredible gift of love offered to us through the life, death, and resurrection of Jesus Christ, our Lord and Savior.

Considering the Concept of Resurrection

You will want to have done a little research on the concept of resurrection and the resurrection of Jesus in order to make a brief presentation on this subject before moving to the next activity, which compares the resurrection narratives in the four Gospels. In your presentation consider mentioning the following points in addition to points you have found in your study:

- Resurrection is not resuscitation of a physical body that died but a total transformation of the whole being of the person.

- There are allusions to resurrection in Isaiah 26:19 as well as in the apocalyptic writing in Daniel 12:1–3.

- On three occasions in Matthew, Jesus speaks of his impending death and says that he "on the third day will be raised" (16:21; 17:23; and 20:19).

- The earliest account of the resurrection of Jesus is not found in the Gospels but in Paul's first letter to the Corinthians, chapter 15. See also Romans 6:5 and Philippians 3:10, 11.

- The resurrection of Jesus is not of his own doing, a final miracle, but is an act of God; it is God who has raised Jesus from the dead.

- The resurrection is more than a miraculous event that happened to Jesus; rather, it is an eschatological event, a turning point in human history.

- The resurrection remains in the realm of mystery.

- Resurrection faith is not based on evidence of an empty tomb but on the experience of the living presence of the risen Christ in the midst of his followers.

Conclude your consideration of the concept of resurrection by a brief discussion of a question or two:

- How do you respond to someone who says, "I think you can be a Christian without believing in the resurrection of Jesus"?

- How important is the resurrection of Jesus to your faith journey?

- What do you think is meant by the phrase "a resurrection faith"?

Comparing Resurrection and Appearances Narratives

In the first few pages of chapter 7 in the Participant's Guide the author writes of the similarities and differences between Matthew's account of the resurrection as compared to the accounts in the other three Gospels. This activity will engage the class in comparing this narrative in the four Gospels. Guide the class with the following directions:

- Turn to page 126 in the Leader's Guide to use the worksheet provided there.

- Form four small groups of equal size, and assign each group a different one of the four Gospels.

- Members of each small group are to read their assigned passage and then answer the eight questions based on their Gospel's account.

- After the small groups have answered the questions, call everyone back to the large group, and then deal with one question at a time by presenting the answer from each of the Gospels.

After all of the answers have been presented by each of the groups, spend a few minutes discussing together one or more of the following questions, or questions you have created.

- When you compare the answers for Matthew with the other three Gospels, what do you notice as the major differences between Matthew and the others?

- What do you see as the common witness of all four Gospels?

- What do you make of the differences in the responses of those who went to the empty tomb?

- What does that suggest to you regarding responses we might make today to the resurrection of Jesus the Christ?

- If you have a favorite among these Gospel narratives, which is it? Why?

Reflecting on the Doctrine of the Trinity

In the Participant's Guide we read, "The Great Commission is also significant for another reason: it contains a clear Trinitarian statement" (p. 65). If you have time, it would be good to spend a few minutes reflecting on the Trinity:

- Begin by asking, "What is your understanding of the Christian doctrine of the Trinity?"

- After participants have shared some of their thoughts, direct them to page 127 in the Leader's Guide, where they will find a list of ten passages that the author suggests are "rudiments of this concept that are found in other New Testament texts."

- Assign one passage to each individual or perhaps pairs.

- Ask them to read the assigned passage and to answer the one question on the worksheet.

- After a few minutes for reading and reflecting on the passages, call the group together and ask them to share what they understand their passage to be suggesting regarding the concept of God the Father, Son, and Holy Spirit.

- When all have shared, lead them to reflect on one more question: How important do you think the doctrine of the Trinity is for Christians today?

- If you have enough time, you could ask how many in the class have memorized the Apostles' Creed. If a good number of the class responds in the affirmative, lead them in reciting the creed.

Evaluating the Course

Take a few minutes with the group to share the following:

- We have spent a number of weeks together studying Matthew's Gospel. We have read the Participant's Guide and many passages in Matthew, have participated in a variety of activities together, and have discussed many questions. It is impossible to remember all we have said and done together, but I am sure there are some things that are memorable from our study. Let's take a few minutes to reflect on our experience of Matthew's Gospel.

- Of all the activities we did together, which ones were the most interesting, challenging, or helpful for you?

- What are some suggestions you would make regarding a future study like this one?

- What are some questions that have been provoked in your mind about the life and ministry of Jesus from the perspective of Matthew's Gospel?

- What are some new insights or learnings that have come to you as a result of this study?

- In terms of your personal faith journey, how has this study contributed to that journey?

- Where do you hope that this study will lead you, our group, and/or our church?

Closing

The last words of Jesus in Matthew's Gospel are known as the Great Commission. The closing for this session and the whole course will be in the form of a commissioning of the class members using the key points of Jesus' commission. Invite everyone to stand and form a circle and, if it is appropriate, to hold hands. You, as the class leader, will speak the phrases from the Great Commission, and the class members will respond. (It would be helpful to print the words of response on large sheets of newsprint.)

Leader: Jesus said, "Go and make disciples of all nations."

Group: *We will go to make disciples.*

Leader: Jesus said, " 'Baptize them in the name of the Father, the Son, and the Holy Spirit.' "

Group: *We will proclaim your good news so others will believe.*

Leader: Jesus said, " 'Teach them to obey everything I have commanded you.' "

Group: *We will teach your word faithfully.*

Leader: Jesus said, " 'Remember, I will be with you always, to the end of the age.' "

Group: *We go believing that Jesus will be with us always.*

Comparing Four Resurrection and Appearances Narratives				
	Matthew 28:1–10	**Mark 16:1–8**	**Luke 24:1–12**	**John 20:1–10**
1. Who went to the tomb?				
2. When did they go to the tomb?				
3. What did they find? Who did they encounter?				
4. What was said to them?				
5. How did they respond emotionally?				
6. What did they do?				
7. How many times did Jesus appear to his followers?				
8. To whom did Jesus appear?				

Reflecting on the Doctrine of the Trinity through Ten New Testament Passages

Instructions: Each person or pair should read and reflect on one of the following passages and then answer the question below.

1. John 1:1–14

2. Romans 8:1–4

3. 1 Corinthians 2:1–5, 10

4. 2 Corinthians 1:18–22

5. Galatians 1:1–5

6. Ephesians 4:1–7

7. Colossians 1:1–20

8. 1 Thessalonians 1:1–6

9. Titus 3:3–7

10. Hebrews 1:1–6

Question:

What does this passage suggest to you regarding the work of God the Father, Son, and Holy Spirit?

Appendix

Commentaries on Matthew

Boring, M. Eugene. *Matthew.* The New Interpreters' Bible, vol. 8. Nashville: Abingdon Press, 1995.

Hagner, Donald. *Matthew 1–13,* Word Biblical Commentary, vol. 33A. Dallas: Word Books, 1993.

_____. *Matthew 14–28,* Word Biblical Commentary, vol. 33B. Dallas: Word Books, 1995.

Herzog, William R. III. *Prophet and Teacher, an Introduction to the Historical Jesus.* Louisville, KY: Westminster John Knox Press, 2005.

Luz, Ulrich. *Matthew 1–7*, Hermenia. Minneapolis: Fortress Press, 2007.

_____. *Matthew 8–20*, Hermenia. Minneapolis: Fortress Press, 2001.

_____. *Matthew 21–28*, Hermenia. Minneapolis: Fortress Press, 2005.

Other Resources on Matthew

Barclay, William. *The Beatitudes and the Lord's Prayer for Everyman.* New York: Harper & Row, 1964.

_____. *Introducing the Bible.* Nashville: Abingdon Press, 1972, 1979.

Betz, Hans Dieter. *The Sermon on the Mount.* Hermenia. Minneapolis: Fortress Press, 1995.

Brown, Raymond E. *An Adult Christ at Christmas: Essays on Three Biblical Stories,* Collegeville, MN: Liturgical Press, 1977.

Carter, Warren. *Matthew and Empire: Initial Exploration.* Harrisburg, PA: Trinity Press International, 2001.

_____. *Matthew and the Margins: A Sociopolitical and Religious Reading.* Maryknoll, NY: Orbis Books, 2000.

Oakman, Donald E. *Jesus and the Peasants.* Eugene, OR: Cascade Books, 2008.

Bible Study Aids

Achtemeier, Paul J., gen. ed. *The HarperCollins Bible Dictionary.* San Francisco: HarperCollins Publishers in consultation with the Society of Biblical Literature, 1996.

Mays, James L., gen. ed. *The HarperCollins Bible Commentary.* Rev. ed., San Francisco: HarperCollins Publishers in consultation with the Society of Biblical Literature, 2000.

Throckmorton, Burton H., ed. *Gospel Parallels: A Comparison of the Synoptic Gospels.* 5th ed. Nashville: Thomas Nelson Publishers, 1992.

Study Bibles

The Access Bible (NRSV). New York: Oxford University Press, 1999.

> Features include introductory articles for each book of the Bible; sidebar essays, maps, and charts in places appropriate to the text; section-by-section commentaries on the text; a glossary; a brief concordance; and a section of Bible maps in color.

The Discipleship Study Bible with Apocrypha (NRSV). Louisville, KY: Westminster John Knox Press, 2008.

> Features include introductory articles for each book of the Bible, study notes for key portions of each chapter of the Bible, a concise concordance, and helpful maps.

The Learning Bible (CEV). New York: American Bible Society, 2000.

> Features include introductory articles and outlines for each book of the Bible; fifteen background articles and over one hundred miniarticles; charts and timelines; a miniatlas; notes on biblical texts in six categories, each identified by a different color and symbol (geography; people and nations; objects, plants, and animals; ideas and concepts; history and culture; and cross-references); and hundreds of illustrations, photographs, and diagrams in color.

The New Interpreter's Study Bible with Apocrypha (NRSV). Nashville: Abingdon Press, 2003.

> Features include introductory articles for each book of the Bible, extensive textual notes, many excursus essays, helpful glossary, general articles related to biblical authority and interpretation, and colorful maps.

The NIV Study Bible (NIV). Grand Rapids: Zondervan, 1985.

Features include introductory articles and outlines for each book of the Bible; extensive notes for explanation and interpretation of the biblical text on each page; helpful charts, maps, diagrams within the biblical text; an index to subjects; a concise concordance; and a collection of maps in color.